RESOURCE BOOKS FOR TEACHERS

series editor
ALAN MALEY

SELF-ACCESS

Susan Sheerin

Oxford University Press 1989

Oxford University Press
Walton Street, Oxford OX2 6DP

Oxford   New York   Toronto
Delhi   Bombay   Calcutta   Madras   Karachi
Petaling Jaya   Singapore   Hong Kong   Tokyo
Nairobi   Dar es Salaam   Cape Town
Melbourne   Auckland

and associated companies in
Berlin   Ibadan

Oxford, Oxford English and the *Oxford English*
logo are trade marks of Oxford University Press

ISBN 0 19 437099 2

Set by Pentacor Ltd, High Wycombe, Bucks

Printed in Hong Kong

Acknowledgements

The author would like to thank her colleagues at the Bell School, Cambridge, for their help and support in this project. In particular, her thanks are due to Judy McCall, Senior Librarian, for her advice and comments on the 'Getting started' section of this book, and to Roger Gower, Principal, for his constant encouragement.

The publisher would also like to thank the following for their permission to use copyright material:

Cambridge University Press for extracts from *Ship or Sheep?* by Anne Baker, *Reading Choices* by David Jolly, *English Pronunciation Illustrated* by John Trim, *Elements of Pronunciation* by Colin Mortimer, and *Learning to Learn English* by G Ellis and B Sinclair; David Cobb for the maps on pp. 147–8; Jonathan Cape and Penguin Books for an extract from *The Wonderful World of Henry Sugar* by Roald Dahl; Andre Deutsch Ltd. for an extract from *After Leaving Mr Mackenzie* by Jean Rhys; Heinemann Educational Books Ltd. for extracts from *The Sign of Four* by Sir Arthur Conan Doyle (retold by Anne Collins), *Teaching Written English* by Ron White, and *Reading Links* by Marion Geddes and Gill Sturtridge; William Heinemann and Doubleday Publishing Co. for an extract from *The Moon and Sixpence* by W Somerset Maugham; Tom McArthur for an extract from *Using English Suffixes and Prefixes* (Collins); Longman Group UK Ltd. for extracts from *Fast Food* by Lewis Jones, *Teaching Writing Skills* by Donn Byrne, and *Britain Since 1700* by R J Cootes and L E Snellgrove; James Nisbet & Co. Ltd. for an extract from *Learn to Spell* by Walter Dawson Wright; Oxford University Press for extracts from *Spotlight on Britain* by S Sheerin, J Seath and G White; *Use Your Dictionary* by Adrian Underhill, and *Idioms in Practice* by Jennifer Seidl; Simon Schuster for an extract from *Approaches to Self-Assessment in Foreign Language Learning* by M Oskarsson.

The Publisher would like to thank Monaco Hang Up Storage Systems, Henley-on-Thames for their permission to reproduce a photograph.

Illustrations by:
Peter Joyce and Oxford Illustrators.

Location photography:
Paul Hutley.

The Publisher has been unable to trace the following copyright holders and would like to hear from them:

Consumer News, issue 8 (extract from 'Superman versus Smoking'); Susan Meredith, Ann Goldman and Tom Lissauer (extract from *The Young Scientist of the Human Body*).

Contents

4 Productive skills 89

The author and series editor

Susan Sheerin started her teaching career as a secondary school modern languages teacher, but soon became interested in teaching English as a Foreign Language. She retrained, taking an RSA Diploma in TEFL/TESL, and then from 1978 taught and directed ESP and teacher training courses at the Colchester English Study Centre. In 1982 she took up the post of Materials Co-ordinator at CESC and was responsible in this capacity for managing teaching and learning resources in the centre, including the library and learning centre. In 1984/5 she took a year's leave of absence to study for an MA in Applied Linguistics at Essex University. In 1986 she was appointed Director of Studies of the Bell School, Cambridge, where among other things the author is closely associated with and has responsibility for the self-access facility in the school. She is co-author of *Spotlight on Britain* (OUP 1985).

Alan Maley worked for The British Council from 1962–1988, serving as English Language Officer in Yugoslavia, Ghana, Italy, France, and China, and as Regional Representative for The British Council in South India (Madras). He is currently Director-General of the Bell Educational Trust, Cambridge.

He wrote *Quartet* (with Françoise Grellet and Wim Welsing, OUP 1982). He has also written *Beyond Words, Sounds Interesting, Sounds Intriguing, Words, Variations on a Theme,* and *Drama Techniques in Language Learning* (all with Alan Duff), *The Mind's Eye* (with Françoise Grellet and Alan Duff), and *Learning to Listen* and *Poem into Poem* (with Sandra Moulding). He is also Series Editor for the Oxford Supplementary Skills Series.

Foreword

The movement for learner independence springs from the powerful yet commonsense perception that it is *learners* who do the learning. (Teachers, however good, cannot do it for them.) It is strengthened by the further observation that every learner is different from every other learner. Disillusionment with 'lockstep' teaching and the development of a communicative/humanistic teaching philosophy which has shifted the focus from teachers to learners have given added impetus to the movement.

The early days of learner independence were characterized by much terminological debate. What exactly was meant by 'autonomy', 'self-directed learning', 'individualization', etc.? These concerns seem now to have been superceded by the more urgent practical need to develop effective mechanisms for allowing students a degree of choice and for helping them to exercise it.

This book describes one such mechanism: The Self-Access Study Centre. Such centres offer students the opportunity to pursue their learning in their own preferred way and at their own pace. They need, however, to be carefully conceived so as to offer a systematically-designed framework of support for the student. Thought has also to be given to organizational systems which integrate the work done in the Study Centre with that done in the classroom or elsewhere.

This book offers highly practical advice, supported by examples of materials, and thus provides invaluable information for anyone considering setting up a self-access facility, however modest.

Alan Maley

Introduction

What is self-access?

This book aims to help EFL (English as a Foreign Language) and ESL (English as a Second Language) teachers with the practicalities of setting up and managing self-access study facilities. The primary aim of such facilities is to enable learning to take place independently of teaching. Students are able to choose and use self-access material on their own and the material gives them the ability to correct or assess their own performance. By using such a self-access facility, students are able to direct their own learning.

At first glance it may appear that providing self-access facilities amounts to a conspiracy to rid the world of teachers, but this is certainly not the case. This book assumes that self-access learning takes place in conjunction with classroom learning and is complementary to it.

Why bother to set up self-access?

Any attempt to cater more for the individual needs of students inevitably means a lot of hard work and effort on the part of teachers in terms of the provision of material and in the general change of attitude and approach required. It is no easy option. On the contrary 'It takes better teachers to focus on the learner', Strevens (1980). No teacher will undertake such a commitment lightly, and it is therefore appropriate to consider the reasons which might make individualization and the provision of self-access facilities worth all the trouble involved.

Learner independence/responsibility

Society teaches us that we need to be taught, i.e. that learning is dependent upon being taught. It does this by the traditional roles that are assigned to teachers and students, whereby the teacher is in tight control, transmitting content and knowledge, selecting and directing activities. Learning and the correction of errors are the teacher's responsibility. The student, on the other hand, is passive, led by the teacher, marching in lock-step with others. Learning is not his or her responsibility. Thus, these traditional roles foster an insidious lack of independence and responsibility in the student. This is liable to hinder learning because of lack of involvement and self-investment in the learning process on the part of the student. Naiman *et al.* (1978) in their study of the characteristics of good language learners, found that the most successful language learning strategies are connected with assuming responsibility for one's own learning.

Teachers cannot learn for students, and in order to increase learner independence and responsibility for learning, the traditional roles need to change as follows, Stevick (1976):

Teacher
paternal/assertive   → fraternal/permissive
dispenser of all knowledge   → resource person/consultant
fostering dependence   → training for independence

Student
passive   → active
no responsibility for learning   → assume responsibility for learning
seeking approval   → doing without overt approval
submissive   → involved in decision-making

Learning to learn

Many educators argue that our world is changing so rapidly that some people may need to retrain several times during their working life due to the need either to keep abreast of developments in their occupation, or to change a redundant occupation for a new, non-redundant one. According to this view, life should be seen as a continuing process of education. The following view is expressed by Carl Rogers (1969):

> Teaching and imparting of knowledge makes sense in an unchanging environment. This is why it has been an unquestioned function for centuries. But if there is one truth about modern man, it is that he lives in an environment which is *continually* changing . . . We are, in my view, faced with an entirely new situation in education where the goal of education, if we are to survive, is the *facilitation of change and learning*. The only man who is educated is the man who has learned how to learn; the man who has learned how to adapt and change; the man who has realized that no knowledge is secure, that only the process of *seeking* knowledge gives a basis for security. (Rogers's emphasis)

If this is the case, there is a radical need to equip people with the tools for undertaking their own learning.

Learners are individuals

Influenced by humanistic psychology, educators have recently emphasized the fact that students are individuals with different needs, styles and interests, and that we as educators and fellow human beings should take account of these differences in the provision made for their learning.

1 Psychological differences

There are psychological differences between students. They differ
in their cognitive abilities and language learning aptitude: some
people learn languages more quickly and easily than others.
They differ in their learning styles, i.e. in their preferred ways
of processing information: some are predominantly auditory
channel learners while others are visual learners; in some
students the left brain is dominant (favouring logical, analytic
thinking), while in others the right brain holds sway (favouring
creative, lateral thinking), and there are many other possible
differences.

2 Study habits

Individuals also differ in their study habits, in their likes and
dislikes of particular learning tasks and activities, in their preferred
skills and in their general problem-solving strategies. Rodgers
'Strategies for individualized language learning and teaching'
(1978) includes the following in his list of individual differences:

- students learn through different media (textbooks, films, games,
  physical activities, etc.)
- students learn through different styles of content/process
  organization (deductive, inductive, discovery, learning by doing,
  memorization, etc.)
- students perform differently in different group arrangements
  (working alone, peer tutoring, small group activities, whole class
  instruction, etc.)
- students' learning efficiency varies differentially according to
  time of study (longer versus shorter study periods, morning
  versus afternoon, beginning of class period versus end of class
  period, first term versus last term, etc.)
- students' learning efficiency varies differentially according to
  place of study (in-class study, library study, laboratory study,
  home study, etc.)

3 Personality differences

Individuals clearly differ enormously also in their personalities,
beliefs, and attitudes. The list of personality and affective variables
appears endless. Just three of the possible variables are:

- the degree of introversion/extroversion (extroverted people tend
  to be more sociable and outgoing, which some researchers believe
  to be desirable qualities for language learning)
- the degree of tolerance of ambiguity (Naiman *et al.* find that this
  tends to be a hallmark of a good language learner)
- the degree of ethnocentricity, i.e. the degree to which one is
  bound to the central tenets or mores of one's culture (good
  language learners tend to have a low degree of ethnocentricity).

4 Motivation

Perhaps the most discussed and examined difference among
students is the varying degree of motivation to learn a language.

This is bound up with attitudes towards the target language and culture, and also related to individual goals and achievement orientation. What is certain is that, especially among adults, there are many different reasons why an individual may wish to learn a foreign language. Some institutional settings may favour one kind of motivation but may be a frustrating and demotivating setting for students with a different kind of motivation.

5 Different purposes

Students have different purposes in learning English. They may be responding to the needs of their job or occupation (future or actual). They may be responding to the necessity of studying in an English-speaking environment or they may be preparing for public examinations in English. They may be learning English because they are immigrants in an English-speaking culture, or they may want to learn English in order to visit an English-speaking country as a tourist. All of these are very specific language-learning purposes. The varied demands of ESP (English for Specific Purposes) students inevitably involve at least some degree of individualization.

6 Summary

The evidence for the existence of psychological, personality, and motivational differences between students is overwhelming and it is this, perhaps, more than anything which provides one of the strongest reasons for introducing some measure of individualized instruction in order to cater for, and indeed exploit, these differences. Instruction consisting of one diet for all aimed at a class of, say thirty, will almost certainly not constitute a completely suitable diet for any one of the individuals in that class.

Language teaching

In addition to psychological and motivational differences, language teachers know to their cost that students differ in the order in which they acquire 'bits' of the language. Many classes are made up of individuals who have followed different syllabuses, and/or have been taught different things by different methods. Even in a class where all individuals have had the same diet from the start, there will be differences in what has been acquired and what not. This manifests itself in the fact that different students, even in a monolingual group, make different sorts of errors.

Errors are no longer regarded as evidence of failure on the part of the student but as valuable evidence for the state of their interlanguage. Many teachers now regard themselves as diagnosticians as well as clinicians, pin-pointing the source of errors and instigating remedial action. This capacity for specific diagnosis of a student's errors is pointless unless the remedial action is directed towards the student and his or her error, i.e. individualized. After all, doctors would not administer insulin to an entire hospital ward because one of the patients was diabetic.

To sum up, self-access learning is the practical solution to many language teaching problems: mixed-ability classes, students with different backgrounds and needs, psychological and personality differences between students, etc. The essential prerequisite to self-access learning is the provision of self-access materials within an organized framework so that students can get at what they need.

Setting up self-access – possible problems

Apart from the enormity of the task of setting up self-access facilities and the practical problems this entails, there can be other less tangible problems in the attitudes and prejudices of teachers and/or students. Let us take the problems of teachers first.

Most teachers have been trained and gained their experience in the traditional mode. A change in role from 'parent' to 'equal' necessitates a change in attitude which can be quite traumatic. Teachers can find, if they are honest with themselves, that they need their students to need them. They may complain about having to chase this student for his or her homework or about having to chivvy that student to arrive punctually, but in reality they can be hooked on this parent-type role. It may be a fundamental part of their self-image, their *raison d'etre*.

Students also have their hang-ups! It is much easier to be dependent and let someone else (i.e. the teacher) take the responsibility. This is the way most educational systems work and it is, therefore, what most students are used to. Cultural differences may also present serious problems. Independence is not a virtue in all cultures. Other qualities of respect, obedience, and self-effacement may be much more highly valued. Moreover, in some religions, people are taught to regard the teacher as an almost mystical figure to be held in awe. He or she is the unquestioned dispenser of knowledge. For students from such a culture, our obsession with independence must seem incomprehensible.

For some teachers and students, a minority, one hopes, it may be useless to try to change ingrained attitudes. For the majority, however, a period of training and development can go a long way towards achieving acceptance of new roles and methods. The question of learner training and development is dealt with in some detail in Chapter 2 – 'Ways in and through'. The issue of teacher training for self-access learning lies outside the scope of this book. Suffice it to say that attention needs to be paid to preparing teachers just as much as students. Training is needed in such areas as student counselling, needs analysis, resources management, etc. Mutual support groups or teacher development groups, where teachers can just talk about their problems to each other, can be a tremendous help. It also helps if teachers are involved right from the start in the whole process of setting up self-access facilities.

How to use this book

This book is intended for teachers and resource centre managers who wish to provide their students with the opportunity for greater independence and choice in their learning. Central to this aim is the provision of suitable self-access material, and so the main body of this book sets out many concrete ideas and suggestions.

Teachers in a wide variety of types of institutions should find this book helpful, ranging from the institution with large resources at its disposal to the small school where resources are limited or poor. It will be useful for those wishing to set up or improve a study centre, but equally there are plenty of ideas here for those teachers who have no such facility available to them but would like to introduce self-access work into the classroom.

The material in this book has also been written with a large variety of students in mind in terms of age, language level, and educational background, in the firm belief that self-access learning should not be restricted to adults in higher education. The format of the activities and instructions are designed to be clear and simple enough for children and adolescents to use while, at the same time, the content of many of the activities is challenging enough for advanced adult students.

This book is not written with a totally autonomous learning situation in mind. It is presumed that students have access to a teacher's guidance for at least some of the time. Most schools and institutions wishing to provide self-access facilities intend students to use them in conjunction with and as a supplement to classroom-based learning, and teachers provide the vital link between classroom and self-access, which is essential if the facility is to be properly utilized. Most students, too, do not want to be completely abandoned. Professional advice which is available but not imposed need not detract from learner independence.

How the book is organized

The book is divided into five chapters, as follows:

1 Getting started
This chapter contains practical advice on how to set up self-access facilities. It deals with questions of layout, equipment, storage, classification, access and retrieval, orientation, staffing, and materials.

2 Ways in and through
This chapter deals with learner training and preparation for self-access learning. It covers initial orientation to the system, level assessment, and looks at ways of helping students make the most effective use of the facilities in the long term.

3 Receptive skills
This chapter contains suggestions for self-access activities in the skills of reading and listening. The first section on each skill looks at intensive reading or listening activities with short texts, while the second focuses on longer texts.

4 Productive skills
This chapter contains suggestions for self-access activities in the skills of writing and speaking. The first section on each skill deals with the mechanics of written and spoken production, i.e. handwriting, spelling, and punctuation in the writing section, and pronunciation in the speaking section. Following this, there is a progression from relatively controlled to free production, with study guides to help both teachers and students.

5 Building blocks
This chapter contains activities which focus on grammar, vocabulary, and key functional areas.

How each activity is organized

Although the activities in this book can be used as they stand, they are intended primarily as 'prototypes' for different types of self-access activities in different areas. They should, therefore, be regarded as blueprints or recipes for the production of other similar activities at varying levels.

The activities consist of three parts:

1 Pre-task/task
The first part of each activity is intended for the student. Apart from the 'Classification', it can include information on 'Level', 'Age', 'Language group', 'Topic', 'Activity type', and 'Aim'. It will also usually provide advice on 'Preparation', as well as 'Instructions', and a 'Task sheet'.

2 Post-task
The second part of each activity is also intended for the student, but should initially be hidden from view. It can include the sections 'Key', 'Tapescript', and 'Follow-up'.

3 About the task
The final part of each activity is directed at the teacher. It consists mainly of 'Comments' and sometimes includes other suggestions or variations which can be used with students at different levels. It is worth examining the sections in more detail:

Classification

This plays a vital role in enabling users to find what they need from the system (see 'Classification and access' – Chapter 1). For this reason, a classification mark plus a unique number should appear on every piece of material. The classification system used in this book is as follows:

- the first letter indicates the main focus, e.g. R. = Reading
- the two letters after the full stop indicate the type of activity, e.g. CL/ = Cloze text
- the number after the slash is the unique number of that particular piece of material, so an activity marked R.CL/5 would be the fifth cloze text in the Reading section
- level is not included in the classification code but is to be taken as indicated by colour-coding (which cannot be shown in this book).

Level

It must be emphasized that the levels quoted refer only to the particular example given, not to the activity itself. Most of the activities included can easily be adapted to different levels by the selection of easier or simpler texts/activity types.

Age

As with Level, the Age indicated refers only to the particular example. Most activities are adaptable for all ages, depending on the content or topic, etc. chosen.

Language group

Where appropriate and useful, i.e. mainly in the grammar and pronunciation sections, the 'Language group(s)' who would most benefit from a particular activity is indicated (see 4.18).

Topic

The topic of a particular activity is shown if it seems to be something that students might conceivably search for when looking for self-access material. Longer reading and listening texts should always be classified by topic.

Activity type

A wide variety of activity types has been included in order to show students the range of tasks which can be done on self-access such as:

- practice/testing activities, e.g. exercises, dictation, cloze texts
- learning/awareness-raising activities, e.g. discovery tasks, information guides, study guides
- reflective/creative activities, e.g. reactive listening, book reviewing, story writing
- social/peer matching activities, e.g. communication tasks.

Aim

Each activity has its aim clearly stated for the student. This is important both from the point of view of motivation, and also in enabling the student to make an informed decision about whether a particular activity is appropriate to his or her needs.

Preparation
This section provides an opportunity for various kinds of learner preparation for the activity to follow such as:

- a focus on vocabulary, setting the scene, 'tuning in' prior to reading, e.g. 3.4; listening, e.g. 3.10; or free writing, e.g. 4.15
- reassurance prior to an apparently difficult or unusual activity, e.g. 3.2 and 3.17
- awareness-raising about the language, drawing attention to native speaker usage, e.g. 4.10
- checking students have the requisite knowledge, suggesting activities they can do to obtain that knowledge, e.g. 4.19
- giving information/prerequisite knowledge for the activity, e.g. 4.20 and 4.21
- organization, instructions to find equipment, etc. e.g. 3.14.

Instructions
The instructions are set out separately from the actual activity for the sake of clarity.

Task sheet
The task sheet contains the main part of the activity: text, various types of questions, etc.

Key
The key contains the answers to activities, the solutions to problems, etc.

Tapescript
If listening material is involved, the tapescript of the listening texts should be stored with the Key.

Follow-up
The follow-up section contains suggestions to the student for further activities or advice on 'where to go from here'. This advice can be of a very general nature, or it can be a specific reference to other activities in the self-access system. Together, the 'Preparation' and 'Follow-up' sections offer the possibility of built-in 'pathways through the system' (see 'Pathways' – Chapter 2).

Comments to the teacher
This section is addressed to the teacher and contains such things as notes on organization of the activity, comments on pedagogic aspects, sources of further similar material, etc. Also included, if appropriate, are variations on the main task.

1 Getting started

Introduction

If you teach in a school which wishes to introduce self-access facilities where previously none existed, then the most fundamental decision which has to be taken initially concerns the location of these facilities. Can the school give up a room or an area which can be used as a study centre with self-access facilities? If this is impossible then other solutions have to be found.

The first section of this chapter is addressed primarily to those who wish to set up or improve a study centre with self-access facilities. Following this, other ways of offering self-access are considered for those teachers or institutions where there is no specially dedicated area or separate room. Generally applicable questions of materials design, classification, and storage are then considered and, finally, there is a look at staffing implications.

Setting up a study centre

The first question concerns the location of the study centre. Which room or rooms is to be given over to this purpose? If your school or institution has a library, then one practical solution is to redesign it so that opportunities for private study using a variety of media are created. In an ideal world a study centre would include a library section and a self-access section.

1 A library section

This section can house books, newspapers, and magazines which cater for a variety of student needs. Apart from the obvious overall need to learn more about English, students may also need to practise study-skills and reference-skills, to gather information for projects or for personal interest, to read extensively for pleasure and for language improvement, to keep abreast of the news, etc. In order to satisfy all these needs, the library could include:

- *a reference section*: dictionaries, grammar books, encyclopaedias, an atlas, etc.
- *a reading section*: simplified readers, light fiction, literature
- **a non-fiction section*: e.g. Britain and USA, travel, biography, etc.
- *newspapers and magazines*: English language newspapers (e.g. one quality, one popular), English language periodicals (e.g. *Newsweek*), EFL magazines
- *an EFL section*: e.g. language workbooks + key, comprehension books + key, ESP and/or EAP books, if appropriate.

*It is obviously necessary to be highly selective here as an EFL school library should not try to rival a municipal or college library. Rather than attempt to be fully comprehensive, decide on a small number of very useful categories which you know will be of interest to your students. Within those categories books should be selected on the principle of quality rather than quantity. Remember to include some simplified non-fiction readers for the lower levels.

2 A self-access section

This section should contain language learning materials which students can use on their own. In order for it to be self-access, students have to be able to find material easily which is at their level and satisfies their perceived needs. They also need to be able to evaluate their own work by checking what they have done against a key or a model answer, or they need to be able to gain some other form of feedback.

If learning material with the same main focus is grouped together (see the section on 'Classification and access' in this chapter), then a self-access section could well comprise:

Reading

preparation, intensive reading/short texts, extensive reading/ longer texts, text types (e.g. jokes)

Listening

preparation, intensive listening/short texts, extensive listening/ longer texts, text types (e.g. songs)

Writing

preparation, handwriting, spelling and punctuation, controlled activities, guided writing activities, free writing topics, text types (e.g. letters)

Speaking

preparation, pronunciation/sounds, pronunciation/stress, etc., communication tasks, games, problem-solving activities, text types (e.g. plays)

Grammar

preparation, verbs, nouns/pronouns, adjectives, adverbs, articles etc., prepositions

Vocabulary

preparation, dictionary work, text-based work, topic-based work, idiomatic language, word building, word associations, self-testing

Social English

preparation, requests, apologies, suggestions, etc.

The organization set out above reflects the organization of materials in Chapters 3, 4, and 5. This is not the only possibility, but is offered as an example of a system that teachers can tailor to the needs of their particular teaching situation. The issues connected with more specialist provision are considered later in this section.

3 Equipment

Although it is possible to set up a useful self-access centre without any technical equipment, if the school has the necessary resources then such equipment, even if it consists of nothing more than a few cassette recorders, can greatly increase the scope of what is offered to students. Here is a list of equipment which can be usefully provided in a self-access study centre (the first item is undoubtedly the most necessary):

Cassette recorders
For listening practice. They should be fitted with earphones (so as not to disturb other students) and, if possible, be wall-mounted so as to leave the desk area free for books and papers.

Audio-active comparative (AAC) Labs
For students to record and listen to their own voice. If this facility is provided, then thought needs to be given to installing sound-proof booths or partitioning off a section of the study centre.

Computers
Computers are an excellent aid to self-access language work, in that they operate as if they had endless patience in pointing out students' errors and giving them instantaneous feedback. They can also generate tests and exercises, a task which teachers find very tedious. Areas for which software is available include:

- *Vocabulary programs*: programs which focus primarily on individual lexical items tend to be presented in game form, and include spelling, anagram, and odd-word-out games. Many of these programs are authorable, that is to say that teachers (or students) can enter their own lists of words which the computer will then use to generate a number of different vocabulary games. *Vocab* (1985) is an excellent example of this kind of software.
- *Text reconstruction programs*: these programs require the student to restore a complete text or parts of a text. This frequently involves the student in making educated guesses on contextual or syntactic grounds. If the guess is correct, then that part of the text is restored. Some of these programs are authorable, that is to say that teachers can type in new texts for the program to operate on. *Quartext* (1985) is a useful piece of software of this type.
- *Test programs*: testing software tends to be very popular with students, who seem to enjoy the challenge of a test when there is no possibility of a poor result causing them to lose face or earn a

teacher's disapproval. Once again, much of the software that falls
into this category includes an authoring facility. *Choicemaster*
(1986) is an extremely popular test program.

- *Adventures*: adventure programs present a fantasy micro-world in
which the user moves from location to location, making
decisions, and carrying out various tasks. One of the most useful
programs of this type for the EFL student is *London Adventure*
(1986).

- *Word processing programs*: the provision of word processing
facilities can help students improve the quality of their written
composition. Dictionary and thesaurus facilities available with
many word processing programs enable students to check their
spelling and they even list alternative words a student could use.
The great ease with which changes can be made to text which has
been already written also encourages students to edit what they
have produced to a much higher standard.

There are other uses for computers in self-access work and for a
more comprehensive treatment of the subject, including listings
and descriptions of software available, the following books are
recommended: *Computers in the Language Classroom* by C Jones and
S Fortesque (1987), and *CALL* by David Hardisty and Scott
Windeatt, in this series, (1989).

Information is also available from the English Language Services
Department of The British Council, 10 Spring Gardens, London
SW1A 2BN, and from CILT.

Video stations
Video is extremely valuable for self-access work. It is a motivating
way of providing information, listening practice, and exposure to
native speakers speaking English (see the section on 'Sources for
extensive listening material' in Chapter 3 for information on
purchasing video material or recording it off-air).

If your institution possesses a video camera, then students
themselves can be recorded. This opens up the possibility of
students video-recording short talks on topics which new students
would find useful and interesting such as: 'Why I have found the
self-access centre useful'; 'English language books I have enjoyed
reading'; or, for UK based institutions, 'The best places to eat near
the school'; 'Interesting places to visit near the school', etc. (For
some creative ideas on using video see *Video* by Cooper *et al.* in this
series).

As well as a video play-back machine and a monitor for viewing, it
is necessary to provide headphones in a self-access centre so that
other students are not disturbed. It is a good idea, in fact, to plug
two sets of headphones into each available video station. Not only
does this double the number of students who can avail themselves

of the facility at any one time, but it also encourages co-operation and communication between students.

If there is to be a fair amount of technical equipment, or if the school may expand in this direction, then it is worth thinking of installing electro-tracking along the wall just above table height. This enables electrical equipment to be plugged in at practically any point along the working surface. Trailing wires are thus kept to a minimum.

4 Layout

When considering the layout of a study centre, the size of the room or area obviously plays a crucial role. If one fairly largish room is available, then it can be divided into convenient sections relating to the various kinds of activities which will be taking place. Careful thought needs to be given to the organization of space available. Needless to say, as well as housing books, self-access materials, and equipment, you need to provide working areas for private study. Provide as much privacy as possible by breaking up large areas into smaller ones, using bookshelves as partitions and screens.

There are also various ergonomic aspects to consider. The movement of people into, through, and out of the study centre needs to be easy and unhindered. This is best achieved by having a central aisle right through the study centre with side bays off. This allows easy movement rather than the tortuous progression which can be induced by maze-type layouts.

Another ergonomic aspect to consider is the distribution of noise. The noisiest part of any library or study centre is inevitably the entrance area, and so activities which involve talking, such as the lending and returning of books, audio-active labs., etc. should be grouped near the entrance so that the study centre becomes progressively quieter as you progress into it, with the most studious activities located as far away from the entrance as possible.

Below is the floor plan of a large purpose-built study-centre which was designed with these points in mind:

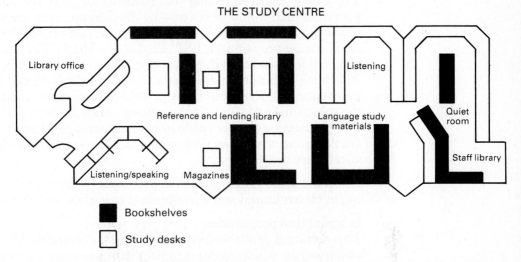

THE STUDY CENTRE

For those with less space at their disposal, here is a suggested layout for a room twelve metres by seven metres:

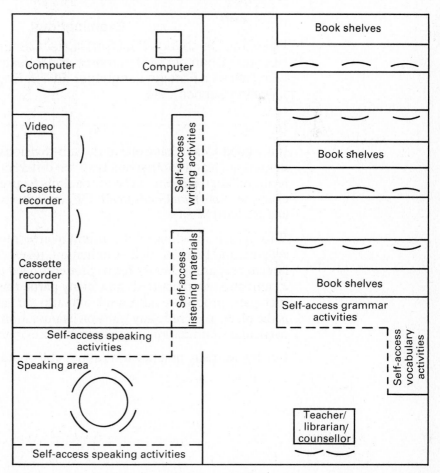

5 More specialized self-access facilities

There may be a need among your students for more specialized provision than would be covered by the common core areas referred to above. There may be a need, for example, for sections on examination preparation, ESP (English for Special Purposes), EAP (English for Academic Purposes), British or American life, etc. This book does not include materials specifically designed for these more specialist areas, but many of the activities can be adapted by the substitution of specialized, authentic texts in the reading and listening sections, more specialized tasks, topics and genres in the speaking and writing sections, and specialized vocabulary in the vocabulary section.

Below are some suggestions as to how some of the specialized areas might be structured and what kinds of materials could be included:

Examination preparation
This section is probably best sub-divided according to the examinations which students in your institution need to prepare for, and the following list is intended merely as an example:

Examinations

general, Cambridge First Certificate, Cambridge Proficiency, London Chamber of Commerce and Industry, TOEFL (Test of English as a Foreign Language), ELTS (English Language Testing Service), etc.

It is a good idea to have one of the sub-divisions devoted to general matters such as a comparison between different examinations in terms of language aimed at and the skills focused on (see, for example, *Longman Guide to ELT Examinations* by Susan Davies and Richard West).

Within each sub-division it is useful to give information on the syllabus and focus of each examination, together with advice on how to prepare and work for it. Students need to know how the examination is structured: how many parts, time allowances for each part, procedure, allocation of marks for each section, etc. This is the place to include any hints on examination techniques for the particular examination in question, advice on timing, etc.

Finally, as many practice tests as possible should be included.

ESP (English for Special Purposes)

The most obvious way to sub-divide an ESP section is according to broad areas of specialism. The areas included will reflect the needs of your institution. The following list is offered as an example:

ESP

business, engineering, science and technology, telecommunications, medicine, hotel and catering, etc.

Within many of the broad areas it will be necessary to have further sub-divisions, e.g. within medicine it may be necessary to distinguish between nurses, doctors, etc. and also between specialisms such as neurology, cardiology, surgery, etc. Because of the need to have sub-divisions within sub-divisions there is a particular need in the area of ESP for an effective classification and indexing system. One possibility is to use a similar system to the one described for the Grammar section in Chapter 5, whereby the numbers are used to denote the sub-divisions within the broad areas, e.g. ESP (English for Special Purposes)

- ESP.MED Medicine
  - ESP.MED1   Cardiology
  - ESP.MED2   Neurology
  - ESP.MED3   Surgery, etc.
- ESP.ENG Engineering
  - ESP.ENG1   Civil Engineering, etc.

It is a good idea to have a general section within each specialist area where generally applicable language areas for that specialism can be focused on, e.g. under ESP.MED for Medicine (without a number denoting a specialty within medicine) it may be appropriate to focus on verb forms for talking about the past and relating past events to the present. This would be relevant for medical practitioners from a wide range of specialties so that they can accurately enquire about or describe the onset and progression of an illness. A comparably generalizable focus for engineering (ESP.ENG) might be such notional areas as 'shapes', 'dimensions', 'properties', etc. (see *Defining and Verbalising* by Mark Fletcher and Roger Hargreaves in the series Functional Units).

Specialist materials should include a large proportion of authentic reading texts and listening materials, and students themselves could make a very valuable contribution in this area by providing examples of texts which they actually have to work with. In addition, there is a large amount of published ESP material which can be adapted for self-access. Some useful materials are:

- Major series:
  Heinemann – *Science and Technical Readers*
  Longman – *Nucleus – English for Science and Technology*
  Longman – *Business English Skills*
  Macmillan – *Career English Series*
  Prentice Hall – *Developing Reading Skills in ESP*
  OUP – *English in Focus Series*
- Videos: business and commerce
  BBC – *Bid for Power*
  Filmscan – *English in Enterprise* (10 case studies)
  Longman – *Visitron – The Language of Presentations*
  Longman – *Visitron – The Language of Meetings and Negotiations*
- Videos: science and technology
  BBC – *The Carsat Crisis*
- Dictionaries
  Longman Illustrated Dictionaries of Science

EAP (English for Academic Purposes)
An EAP section can be organized according to academic skills, as in
the following example:

EAP

reference skills, seminar skills, listening to lectures, academic
reading, academic writing, etc.

(If this form of organization is chosen, then the content of the
materials will tend to be of general rather than specialist interest,
i.e. covering topics such as pollution, conservation, social problems
such as drug addiction, etc. An alternative way of organizing the
EAP section, which may be more appropriate for the language
support units of universities, is to have a section where academic
skills would be covered in general terms, followed by work on
specialist areas such as economics, Third World studies, etc.)

Here are some ideas for material to be included in the sub-sections:
- Reference skills: this section would consist of discovery tasks and
  study guides on such areas as the use of the library and its
  facilities, including how to use the card indexes, how to request a
  book both within the home library and on interlibrary loan, how
  to use microfiche, etc.
- Seminar skills: this section could focus on the structuring and
  delivery of oral presentations and on the common functions of
  discussion such as expressing agreement or disagreement,
  requesting clarification, etc. Suitable materials for raising the

students' linguistic awareness would be audio tapes or videotapes of native-speaker presentations, talks, discussions, etc. and/or audio-recorded or video-recorded presentations of past students (having gained their consent, of course).

– Listening to lectures: the aim of materials in this section would be to help students perceive the overall structure of a lecture, to recognize from verbal and non-verbal cues when a speaker is moving from one topic to another, when a speaker is digressing, and so on. This section would also incorporate study guides and practice in note-taking.

– Academic reading: this section could include study guides on how to use abstracts, contents pages, book indexes, etc. in order to scan and be selective in reading. It would focus on a variety of reading skills such as prediction from titles, chapter headings, sub-headings, etc; identification of key sentences and paragraphs; following a logical argument; recognizing the writer's intentions, etc. This section would also incorporate study guides on effective note-taking from written texts.

– Academic writing: this section could include study guides on how to avoid plagiarism, how to quote and refer to other works in a written text, how to keep and present a bibliography. It should look at cultural norms and expectations in terms of rhetorical structure and style (e.g. British academic writing, unlike that of some cultures, does not tend to draw on proverbs or religious writing such as the Bible, to add weight to an argument). It should also examine the wording of assignments and examination questions, and the sort of response expected by tutors and examiners when they, for example, direct students and examinees to 'discuss'. To this end, model answers can be included together with an analysis and commentary on the structure. At a more detailed level, this section could focus on the expression of discourse functions associated with academic writing such as defining, describing, comparing and contrasting, evaluating, etc.

– Work on specialisms: if you choose to sub-divide according to specialist areas, then issues of classification and indexing are similar to ESP (see above). As in the ESP system, this section would consist mainly of authentic texts from journals and textbooks or recorded lectures and talks, many of which could hopefully be provided by the students themselves. Standard reading and listening exercises for academic texts could be extremely useful in this context.

British/American life and institutions

A focus on British and/or American life may be necessary in a secondary school as the 'culture' component of a modern languages programme. Within institutions in the UK a section on British life may also be relevant for a variety of purposes such as providing orientation to life in Britain and survival skills, or as a basis for special project work which makes use of the environment beyond the school (see Chapter 2). The following list is an example of the categories which could be included:

British institutions

education, government, trade and industry, welfare services, National Health Service, the media, sport and leisure.

Institutions where students wanted to focus in more detail on day-to-day British life would probably include sub-sections like 'Going to the bank', 'Using public transport', etc.

Self-access work in the classroom

If resources are limited, a separate room or study centre of the kind envisaged above may not be feasible. Teachers in this situation need certainly not abandon the idea of individualizing learning and encouraging learner independence and responsibility. There is a lot that can be done in the classroom to change the traditionally dominant role of the teacher and the passive role of the student.

There are ways of turning a classroom into a mini self-access centre once or twice a week or however often seems appropriate. This can be done by setting up semi-permanent activity corners: a listening corner with a couple of cassettes and headphones; a reading corner with a class library and/or a reading laboratory (see the section on 'reading laboratories' in Chapter 3); a games table or cupboard where games with clear instructions for self-access are kept; a computer, if available; another corner with a collection of grammar books, dictionaries, and associated workbooks.

Another possibility is to put together a self-access box (or collection of boxes) or a self-access trolley which could be used all over the school. The attraction of this idea is its flexibility. The relatively small scale of the operation allows sceptical schools and/or teachers to try out self-access learning in a small way. They can then build up their resources as and when necessary, drawing on their experience of the way in which the facility is being used.

As far as practical considerations are concerned, if it is intended to store self-access material in boxes, then one box per level is probably the most convenient method of organization, i.e. a beginners' box, an intermediate box, etc. A system for teachers to book the self-access material for their classes is most useful.

The British Council film, *Activity Days*, indicates yet another way of providing students with self-access facilities in an institution which lacks a dedicated room or area for the purpose. The film shows how, for one day a week over a six-week course for pre-sessional university students, the normal timetable was suspended and students could choose to go to one of four rooms. The four rooms in question were each given over to a different kind of activity and focus for the day. One room contained all the day's newspapers, and tasks relating to the papers were written up on the board. Another room contained a selection of self-access communication games (e.g. 4.25–4.29 in Chapter 4). In the third room, which was equipped as a language laboratory, a variety of self-access listening materials were provided, and in the fourth room students could choose to do study skills-related tasks with a particular emphasis on writing. There was a teacher available for consultation and guidance in each room, and the students were allowed to spend their time in whichever room or number of rooms they wished. Work record cards were given to each student and, on these, information was entered concerning the time of arrival and departure in each of the rooms, and the activities completed there. This model is one which other institutions, which lack space, could consider adapting to their own particular needs.

Materials design and production

1 Criteria for design

What criteria should be applied to the design of good self-access material? Here are some suggestions:

Clearly stated aims
It is extremely important that the student should understand what the aims of the self-access material he or she uses are. This enables the student to decide whether or not it suits his or her needs.

Clarity of rubric
Careful attention should be paid to rubrics when writing or adapting material. If students are going to work on their own there is a need for the utmost clarity, together with clear examples of what is required. It is also necessary to control the level of language used in instructions. If the material is elementary, the rubric should be comprehensible to someone at that level. Another possibility in a monolingual situation, is to write instructions in the students' mother tongue, thus avoiding all misunderstanding.

Attractive presentation
Great care needs to be taken to ensure that self-access materials are as attractive and inviting as possible. Material with a professional finish will give the student confidence.

Worthwhile activity

This seems an obvious point but it is, nevertheless, worth stating that the activity the student is required to do should be worthwhile. That is to say, it should be possible to learn something by doing the activity, and that 'something' should be worth learning (see the 'Design for learning' section below). The material should also be motivating and interesting. People working on their own especially need such a stimulus.

Choice of procedure

Bearing in mind that the purpose of providing self-access facilities is to increase learner independence, materials writers should try not to be unnecessarily dictatorial in the instructions that they write. Offering students a choice of procedure gives them the opportunity to employ learning styles which suit them best (see 3.14–3.16).

Feedback

Self-access materials are used without a teacher, and therefore, feedback needs to be built in. Practice activities need keys; listening material needs a tapescript; more subjective activities require commentaries rather than keys (see 4.23). For free production activities feedback can take the form of successful task performance, 'publication' (see 4.13), or model answers.

Balanced diet

When looked at as a whole, the provision of materials should be balanced and coherent, that is to say the quantity of material at each level and for each main focus should be more or less the same. There should also be a variety of activity types and aims.

2 Design for learning

A generally accepted definition of self-access material tends to be that it consists of activities or text, plus questions or tasks which are self-correcting; that is to say there is only one right answer, so that objective marking is possible. This means that students themselves can correct their own work and they must, therefore, have access to the answer(s) or key.

Self-correcting self-access material basically consists of different types of tests. The feedback which such an activity provides, especially as it is discovered by the students themselves, can lead to learning, but a self-access centre which consists only of such material is providing rather barren fare. The philosophy underlying the introduction of self-access learning is concerned with more than simply shifting the source of all wisdom from a teacher to an answer book or key (provided anyway by teachers). The possibilities are greater than this. Self-access material can inform and generally raise awareness (e.g. discovery tasks, information guides, study guides), lead the student to be reflective and/or creative (e.g. reviewing, story writing), or can encourage the student to join up with his or her peers in order to engage in communication tasks, games, etc.

Even with the traditional practice or testing type of activity there are various ways to place more emphasis on learning:

– students can be guided towards the appropriate section(s) of works of reference such as grammar books and dictionaries if they have answered many questions wrongly

– short explanations can be given as to why the correct answer *is* correct, or incorrect answers are wrong (this tactic is particularly appropriate for use with comprehension work – see 3.2).

3 Using published material

When setting up a system there is obviously a need for the rapid production of a lot of material to form the basis of the self-access centre. For the sake of speed it is best to think in terms of using published material to begin with. Books and workbooks can be cut up (not photocopied, as this would contravene copyright) to form small, self-contained units of work with an identifiable focus. Make sure you adapt the published material to suit your in-house style and standard layout.

For practice or test-type activities any published material which uses exercises or comprehension questions which can be marked objectively, i.e. short factual questions, yes/no questions, true/false questions, multiple choice questions and the like, is potentially suitable for self-access, especially if there is a key to the questions. (If there is no key then someone will have to work out the answers and provide one.)

Published material can usefully be combined with in-house written material. For example, a grammar exercise from a book can be preceded by an introduction and presentation of the grammar point written by one of the teachers. In this way it is possible to aim the material very sensitively at a particular group of students. In monolingual situations this can be particularly useful, and the students' mother tongue can be used for explanations, if necessary.

4 Producing your own material

Once the need for an initial mass of material has been satisfied, then teachers can be encouraged to write original self-access material or adapt their previously written classroom worksheets. In-house produced material is extremely valuable as it is inevitably more precisely geared to the needs of students than published material. Moreover, some of the more interesting activity types (see 'Design for learning' above) are not easily to be found in published form.

If all teachers pool their ideas and material it is possible to build up a reasonable self-access facility which all can use within a much shorter time than if each teacher works in isolation. This is a project which does need co-ordination and the agreeing of clear objectives before materials preparation begins in order to lend coherence and balance to the materials produced. One possibility is to allot to each teacher responsibility for an area that they are interested in e.g. pronunciation, listening, study-skills, etc. so that it is possible for one person at least to have an overview of how each section is developing. If possible, activity types and levels required should also be agreed and worked out beforehand. The clearer the brief, the faster the actual production can proceed. (See also the section on 'Staffing' below.)

Students should be involved in building up the self-access facilities if at all possible and their opinions canvassed on what kind of material is needed and how it should best be organized.

Students can also be encouraged to contribute texts, recordings, songs, advertisements, etc. which have caught their attention. Such materials are a valuable addition to any self-access centre because they reflect the needs and interests of the users as defined by them. In the same way it is also useful to get feedback from students about how they use the centre once it is in operation.

Care needs to be taken to ensure that materials are attractively presented. Where possible, it is desirable for materials to be typed or word-processed, but neat handwritten materials can be perfectly acceptable where other facilities are not easily available. The important thing is to ensure that materials are consistent in terms of classification, layout, and standard headings. In this way a 'professional look' can be achieved even in the absence of sophisticated reprographic facilities.

Classification and access

When deciding on a classification system for self-access materials, the basic principle is to keep it simple. The simpler the system, the easier the access for students.

There are essentially two interrelated questions to consider:
1 How are you going to classify, i.e. what categories will you use?
2 How will students gain access to what they need?

The most basic and necessary classification categories for EFL are *level* and *main focus*, e.g. reading, grammar, etc. Beyond this it is highly desirable to have a few broad sub-divisions of the *main focus*, e.g. verbs, adjectives, nouns, etc. in the grammar section. Another useful classification category is *activity type*, e.g. dictation, game, etc. It is also useful to classify certain materials such as extensive reading and listening texts by *topic* and/or by *text type*.

There are two ways in which students can gain access to self-study material: by browsing or by using a catalogue or card-index.

While those who painstakingly compile the catalogues and card-indexes (see Chapter 5) may wish that more people would use the latter method more often, the fact is that it seems to be human nature to browse, and most students (and teachers?) use this method to locate what they need. That being the case, the sheer physical organization and labelling of the material becomes as important, if not more so, than the catalogues. At this point the question of access needs to be looked at in conjunction with the various classification categories.

Probably the most helpful way to organize the learning material for easy 'browsing' access is by *level* and *main focus*.

1 Level

Material at the appropriate language level is undoubtedly the first requirement for students working on their own, and therefore, if they are to be able to browse, the level needs to be marked clearly on the material itself. This can be done explicitly, i.e. BEG for beginner, INT for intermediate, etc. or with the use of numbers or letters, i.e. 1 = beginner, 2 = elementary, etc. or A = beginner, B = elementary, etc. (If preferred the lowest numbers and first letters can be used for the most advanced levels.) However, perhaps the clearest and most convenient way of marking level is by colour-coding, i.e. blue for beginner, yellow for elementary, etc. This has the great advantage of immediate accessibility to students. Once they know the colour for their level they can see at a glance which material is suitable for them. It also has the advantage of not 'using up' letters or numbers at this stage so that they may be used in the classification system to indicate something else.

2 Main focus

The best way to facilitate access to these categories is actually to group material physically according to main focus so that all the vocabulary material is in one place, all the listening material in another and so on, each section being clearly labelled. If the level of each item is clearly colour-coded, then access to both these categories is very straightforward.

It is also necessary, however, to use a classification code to indicate the focus, and to mark the material with this code. This is necessary if there is to be a catalogue of the main focus areas and also enables the material to be replaced correctly after it has been removed from its location. The classification code can be a number, e.g. 1 = grammar, 2 = vocabulary, etc. but the disadvantage of this is that it can be difficult to learn.

The most straightforward classification for this category is to use letters, namely the first letter of the category, e.g. R = reading, W = writing. The advantage of this system is that numbers can be used to identify a particular item of material within a category.

3 Sub-categories

The introduction of sub-categories within the main focus does complicate matters somewhat but this seems a small price to pay for the increased usefulness to students, in that such sub-categories enable them to search for, say, punctuation or spelling within the Writing section. However, it is advisable to keep the number of sub-divisions to a minimum so that it is easy to keep an overview of the system. One useful sub-category to mark is *activity type*. Another useful sub-category would be sub-focus, e.g. *letters* in Writing (main focus).

The classification mark for the sub-categories can again consist of letters, thus leaving numbers to uniquely mark an item of material within the sub-category. If the main category is indicated by one letter, e.g. L = listening, then the sub-category can be indicated by two or three letters separated from the first letter by a dot, e.g. L.DI indicates a dictation in the Listening section. In order to identify each piece of material in that category, numbers can now be used, e.g. Item L.DI/1, made up as follows:

- L   main focus   = listening
- .DI   activity type   = dictation
- /1   accession   = the first example of this material.

4 Topic

If one has used physical location to indicate the whereabouts of reading, writing material, etc. then obviously such material cannot also be grouped according to topic, so access to topic will have to be through a topic card-index. In a situation, however, where topic is of primary concern, for example, in a school which does a lot of ESP, then there is a very strong argument for grouping material physically according to topic.

In classifying material according to topic it is best to work within a predetermined framework rather than just assign topics as the fancy takes you, because this will tend to lead to a great proliferation of topics, many of which will become too specific and difficult to use. One such open-ended system which the author has encountered produced topics such as 'Clay pots' and 'Camels'. It is unlikely that anyone would actually search for material on these topics, and the function, therefore, becomes purely descriptive. If people are to make efficient use of a topic index to search for material, it is necessary to have a delimited system so that one has an overview and knows what one is likely to be able to find.

Probably the most widely-used topic classification system in the world is the Dewey decimal system. This classification system does not lend itself very easily, however, to the needs of most EFL institutions. It is too detailed in some areas, e.g. philosophy, and not detailed enough in others, e.g. basic lexical areas such as

everyday activities. There is a need for a less formal and academic
system. Appendix 1 contains an extract from a Topic Classification
system specially compiled for use in an EFL situation. It contains a
fairly small number of broad categories which all have sub-
categories within them. (The number of sub-categories can easily
be expanded.) Where material in this book is classified by *topic*, it is
this classification system which has been used, e.g. in 3.9 the topic
is Natural world/Wildlife (birds: Nuthatch).

In this example 'Natural world' is the broad category, and
'Wildlife' is a sub-category. Both these topics could be searched for
in the classification system. '(birds: Nuthatch)' is the specific
topic of this item which would not form part of the classification
system and would be purely descriptive telling you more about the
item you had found under 'Natural world' and/or 'Wildlife'.

5 Indexes

Indexes allow users of a self-access system to search more
specifically for certain types of material than purely physical
location (by, for example, main focus) or colour coding (for level).
Features such as topic, activity type or text type, which may be
ignored for the purposes of physical organization, can be classified
and searched for by means of an index. A computer database can be
very useful for indexing purposes. Computerized classification and
access allows users of the system to search on several dimensions at
once, e.g. for a dictation at lower intermediate level on the topic of
aircraft construction. Computerized databases, as well as enabling
you to search on screen, as it were, will automatically produce cards
for card-indexes, catalogues, or lists of certain kinds of material so
that users do not have to have access to the computer to benefit.

Vocabulary worksheets/Work cards

V1 DICTIONARY USE

'Use Your Dictionary' Chapter 1   V1-601
A guide to the 'Oxford Advanced Learner's Dictionary of Current
English' and the 'Oxford Student's Dictonary of Current English'.
Chapter 1 - The Dictionary Entry   WS (7pp)

V4 VOCABULARY USE

A Family Tree   V4-601
A family tree where you have to work out the relationship
between the people.
From 'Test Your Vocabulary' Book 1 by P Watcyn-Jones   WC

Extract from a computerized database

Materials storage and display

1 Papers and printed material

A lot of work goes into the production of worksheets and instruction sheets, etc. and it is, therefore, worth taking some trouble to ensure that they last as long as possible. To this end sheets of paper can be stuck on to card and laminated, covered in plastic film from a tear-off roll, or stored in plastic envelopes or paper envelopes. Careful storage can increase the life-span of materials that have taken a lot of time and trouble to produce.

Each item (which may consist of a number of pages) can be stored in separate pocket folders, colour-coded for level. (For ease of access, the Key to each item is best stored together with the activity in the same folder. It can either be hidden from view in a separate envelope clearly marked 'Key' or 'Answers', etc. or put on the reverse side of the task sheet.) If activities involve multiple copies of worksheets which students can write on, store these in a separate envelope in the folder, together with instructions to inform a teacher or supervisor when the last one is used. Masters can be filed away in a separate location ready to be photocopied or cyclostyled. If there are no copying facilities available, students will have to copy out worksheets into their own books.

Suitable storage then needs to be found for the pocket folders. Possibilities include: shelves with vertical divisions; open box-like containers, and plastic vertical file boxes (open). Label each different location or section of the study centre clearly and then label each piece of material with its location code so that it is easy to see where to get material and where to put it back. This aspect of display is very important for ease of access by students.

Library supply catalogues are well worth consulting as they contain many useful storage ideas.

2 Cassettes

Cassettes can be stored together in a clear plastic envelope with the printed material which accompanies them. The envelopes can then be hung on rails. This system makes multi-media material easy to use and reduces the chances of misfiling.

Separate storage of cassettes and printed material is also possible, in which case cassettes need to be stored horizontally (so that titles can be read) in open cassette holders so that they are visible and accessible. It should be immediately apparent which printed material goes with which cassette. This can be achieved by allocating the same number and classification code to two or more pieces of material which belong together, and clearly labelling them.

Staffing

It is ironic to think that when the idea of self-access learning was first introduced, there were fears expressed that teachers would become superfluous. In fact, the provision of self-access facilities involves a lot of work, mostly by teachers.

There are three main areas to consider in relation to staffing.

1 Preparing the materials and setting up the system

If an institution is investing in the provision of a study centre, then thought also needs to be given to providing teachers with time to prepare self-access materials to go into the centre. This can be done in a number of ways, of which the following are just examples:

– One or more teachers can be released from some or all of their teaching responsibility for a period of time. Releasing teachers full time has the advantage that they will not be distracted from materials preparation by teaching. On the other hand, teachers should not be kept out of the classroom so long that they begin to lose touch with what students need. If teachers are to be released part-time, the timetable should be arranged so that materials preparation time comes in usable blocks such as whole mornings or whole afternoons rather than the odd hour here and there.

- If the institution has terms or is closed to students at some time during the year, then the entire teaching staff can be employed for a period in the preparation of self-access materials. This has the advantage that a lot of material can be produced in a relatively short period of time and is particularly useful in the initial stages when there is little or no self-access material available. What has been stated above about clear objectives applies just as much in this situation. The difference is that a number of different areas can be tackled at once.
- Material, prepared by teachers in their own time, can be paid for at a given rate per item. With this system it is much easier to calculate a fair rate of remuneration, i.e. based on product rather than production time which may vary tremendously between one teacher and the next. Once again, however, a clear and detailed brief is absolutely necessary for all materials preparation. This is the best safeguard for all concerned.
- Standard reading and listening task sheets can be devised, which are applicable to any text of a particular genre. For example, a standard listening task for use with news broadcasts would focus on those elements common to *all* news broadcasts such as the number and order of the items; who they concern; where they take place; what kind of event is being described; personal reactions to the stories, etc. Standard tasks of this nature not only save on materials writing time, but they focus students' (and teachers'!) attention on the essential qualities of the genre in question. Standard tasks also make it very easy to add or change texts because new worksheets do not have to be written each time. This allows texts to reflect current events and interests of students. Indeed, they can contribute their own texts. (For examples of standard listening and reading tasks see 3.6, 3.17, and 3.18.)
- If resources are limited and there is no time or money available for materials production, a few evening workshops with liquid refreshment on hand can be a relatively painless way of providing an initial base of material and, promoting staff cohesion and solidarity! This may appear to be a Utopian ideal, but if teachers' enthusiasm is fired by an idea such as computer assisted language learning or self-access learning, it is amazing what they can and do achieve in their own time through the formation of self-help groups and the sharing of ideas and materials.

2 Maintaining and adding to the system

Some system of maintenance is required such as a tray or box where users can put faulty tapes and damaged or dilapidated material. Staffing is necessary to oversee such a system, to generally keep the place tidy, check that material is not mis-shelved and to effect repairs as and when necessary. It is also necessary to have someone responsible for the classification, labelling and preparation of new material, and for entering it into the system.

It is also a good idea to keep some kind of statistical check on the use of materials. This can be done by asking students to place folders they have finished using into a tray. The tray is then emptied regularly (at least once a day) by whoever is responsible for supervising the study centre. Before returning the material to its correct place in the system, a tally mark can be made in an unobtrusive place inside the folder. This ensures that the frequency (or lack of it!) with which a particular item is used is recorded and gives valuable feedback to those engaged in stocking up the system. (It also means that there is less chance of material being mis-filed.)

3 Supervision and counselling

If the institution sets up a study centre it is necessary to decide as a matter of policy whether it is to be staffed full-time, part-time, on demand (i.e. a member of staff is on call nearby) or not at all.

There are at least three good reasons why institutions should provide at least part-time staffing for the study centre:

- Students may need guidance initially and from time to time thereafter about how best to use the system, where to find certain material, etc. Although it should be possible for students to use the system completely unaided, in practice this demands quite a high degree of sophistication on the part of the student, even with the simplest and clearest of systems.
- Students will need guidance and counselling to help them analyse their own needs and set their own targets in relation to the system (see the section on 'full and effective use' in Chapter 2). They also need help in evaluating and monitoring their own progress (see 'Setting targets' in Chapter 2).
- Books and materials will disappear through carelessness, thoughtlessness, and dishonesty if the system is totally unsupervised. Not only is this very expensive, it also drastically reduces the efficiency, and reliability of the system.

4 Student involvement

It is a good idea to involve students in the maintenance and administration of their self-access centre. Factors such as the students' age and average length of stay in the institution will determine whether and to what extent such involvement is a practical proposition. If such help can be enlisted, then the advantages are many: students become more self-reliant and responsible, both as a body and as individuals, and they have more opportunities for getting to know the system well, and of influencing its development. In addition, institutions which just cannot afford to pay for the permanent staffing of a self-access centre, may be able to establish a rota system of volunteer student helpers to assist in the running and supervision of the system.

2 Ways in and through

Introduction

The availability of self-access facilities, however excellent they may be, will not in themselves guarantee full and efficient use of those facilities by students. Users need to be shown ways into the system and be guided to make the best use of it in the long term. This kind of guidance is often referred to as 'learner training'.

Some teachers feel disquiet at the concept and/or the term 'learner training', because it seems to betray a patronizing attitude on the part of educators: 'We know the right way to learn and we shall now train you, the student, to follow the one right way.' There are other teachers who point out that some of their students, because of their age and/or their educational and cultural background, do not possess some of the necessary skills to study a language, especially a language which may use a different alphabet to their own.

In considering these two extreme attitudes, it may be useful to distinguish between 'learner training' and 'learner development'. The word 'training' implies the imparting of a defined set of skills, and students may need initial training if certain basic, well-defined skills for language study are lacking. Such basic skills would include the ability to look up items in an alphabetical list; to use a dictionary effectively; to look up a card-index; to use a grammar reference book, etc. If, however, a student is already in possession of the basic skills required, 'learner development' would seem to be a more satisfactory way of describing the process by which that student might come to a deeper understanding of how he or she learns best, and to a greater awareness of what is involved in learning to communicate in a foreign language. 'Training' seems to imply something which is done to the student, whereas 'development' is something the student can do for himself or herself. Learner development materials, then, should aim to offer alternatives and plant seeds, but not impose a particular way of operating on the student.

The activities in the 'Orientation' and 'Basic study skills' sections below are aimed at learner training – they impart a defined set of skills. Most of the other activities in this chapter, however, are more directed towards learner development, as are the study guides later in this book.

Preparation

1 Orientation

Careful thought needs to go into how students are to be orientated to the system when they first arrive. There are, of course, broader issues here concerning why students should be involved in directing their own learning outside the classroom, and how they should set about doing this – areas that need to be tackled through learner training and development – (see 4.13). However, on a more practical level, students first need to physically find their way around a study centre and its classification system. Clear signs on walls and shelves, and labels on material itself play an important role, but there is also a need for an information sheet or study centre guide which can be issued to every student, listing what is available and where to find it. Another excellent idea for initiating students into the system is to give them orientation task sheets to do in which the tasks mirror the kinds of problem the students themselves might face when trying to use the system. Below is an example which, of course, would need to be adapted to specific situations.

2.1 Orientation task

CLASSIFICATION T.OR/1 = Training. Orientation/1

LEVEL All

AGE All

ACTIVITY TYPE Discovery task

AIM To help you get to know the study centre and understand how it is organized so that you can find what you need.

PREPARATION Make sure you have found out what your language level is.

TASK SHEET 1 What is your level, and what colour must you look for: yellow, blue, red, green, pink, or brown?

2 You are looking for information on the British political system. Is there any material on this for you? If so, what is the classification and number of the item? (Remember to check that the colour is right for you.)

3 You need to practise the use of *the* and *a*. Is there any material on this for you? If so, what is the classification and the number of the item? (Remember to check that the colour is right for you.)

4 You want to improve your spoken English. What is the classification and number of the material which gives you advice on this?

5 You need to know how to set out a business letter in English. Is there any material to help you with this? If so, what is the classification and number of the item?

6 You would like to do some work on English idioms. Where would you look?

7 What is the classification and number of the material about 'Sleep'? Explain what the classification and the number mean.

COMMENTARY

1 If you are in any doubt about the correct answer to this question consult your teacher or the librarian.

2 You need to use the 'Topic' card-index to answer this question. Look first for the main category, 'British Life', and then for the sub-category, 'Politics'. If you had difficulty answering this question, look again at the 'Topic' classification system which is on the wall near the 'Topic' card-index.

3 For this you need to look in the Grammar section for the materials marked '*the*, etc.'. There is material on this grammar point at all levels.

4 There is a study guide in the Speaking section entitled 'Improving your spoken English' (4.24) which gives advice on this.

5 For this you need to look in the Writing section under 'Letters'.

6 Work on idioms can be found in the Vocabulary section under 'Idiomatic language'.

7 You need to use the 'Topic' card-index to answer this question. Look first for the main category, 'Personal' and then for the sub-category 'Dreams/Sleep'. The classification for the item on sleep is R.ST/1 which means 'Reading, scrambled text, number 1'.

Comments to the teacher

1 It is worth remembering that new teachers also need orientating to the self-access facilities. A good way of doing this is to have them work through the same orientation task as the students.

2 As a variation, prepare a separate orientation task for each language level.

2 Basic study skills

This section is concerned with minimal 'survival' skills necessary to study a language on one's own. The term 'on one's own' is not intended to convey complete learner autonomy, but describes even those occasions when students are doing set homework out of class and may need to consult a dictionary, a grammar book, or find out information from a library.

Some basic language learning skills, e.g. awareness of grammatical terminology, or how to keep a vocabulary book, seem to belong to a particular section of the self-access centre, e.g. Grammar or Vocabulary, and they are probably best dealt with there. But some language study skills seem more fundamental or more generally applicable than these. They include the ability to order items alphabetically, the ability to use a library index, or to look something up in a contents list or dictionary, etc. These are the sorts of reference skills which students need to master right at the start of any course of study, and you may wish to keep such material all together in a section called 'Study skills', or some such name.

Of all the study skills listed above, effective dictionary use is particularly important for language learning and deserves extensive and detailed treatment. Few students, even advanced ones, know how to distinguish a good dictionary from a bad one, or when it is appropriate to use a monolingual dictionary and when not. Moreover, few students know how to unlock the key to the wealth of information on grammar, pronunciation, and usage contained in a good student's dictionary such as the *Longman Dictionary of Contemporary English* or the *Oxford Advanced Learner's Dictionary* (fourth edition). This is a great pity as a good dictionary is not only an indispensable aid to self-access work, it is something that students can use long after their English course is finished to enable them to continue learning more about English. Both of the dictionaries mentioned above have practice books to accompany them, which can be very easily adapted for self-access work. For lower level students, the *Longman Active Study Dictionary* or the *Oxford Student's Dictionary of Current English* (new edition) both have introductory sections with exercises on finding words quickly, finding two word entries, etc.

Level assessment

Before students can use a self-access centre they need to know what level of that system it is appropriate for them to work at. Levels are not absolute. They vary from one institution to another in their number and division. The understanding of 'Advanced' in one school may be different from another school's understanding of that term. This is immaterial. What the student needs to know is his or her level, not in any absolute sense, but in relation to the system he or she is about to use. There are various ways in which this can be determined.

1 Informal assessment

Students can be assessed informally by teachers on their performance in class over the first few days, and then advised on the level they should look for in self-access.

Advantages
- Informal assessment of this type can work well with a small number of broad levels, i.e. no more than five or six.
- A tutorial relationship is established from the start and the teacher is involved in the students' work outside the classroom.

Disadvantages
- Assessment will be subjective and may be inaccurate.
- Students may be reinforced in their idea that the teacher will tell them what to do – outside the class as well as in it. The responsibility for assessment is taken away from the student.

2 Placement testing

Students can be given a standard placement test such as the Allan, *Oxford Placement Tests* the results of which have been correlated with success at the various levels of self-access material over a period of time. The test should be objective for ease of administration (i.e. multiple choice questions, etc.). The Key to the test and a guide to interpretation can be given to students so that they themselves mark the test and thus notice their own problems.

Advantages
- An objective test may be more reliable.
- Placement testing has 'face validity' for many students. It has the mystique of professionalism about it and they have confidence in the results, and therefore, confidence in using the system.
- The test itself can be used as a way into the self-access system in that the first items students work on could be things they got wrong in the test.

Disadvantages
- Objective assessment of this kind can seem very impersonal.
- Placement testing means increased administrative work. Also, objective tests often favour recognition skills rather than productive ones. Moreover, discrete item tests cannot accurately assess overall communicative competence.

3 Self-assessment

Students can be invited to assess themselves on a sliding scale of, say, 1 to 5, if they are given some idea of the meaning of, at the very least, the upper and lower reaches of the scale. Below are two examples of self-assessment forms for listening taken from Oskarsson, *Approaches to Self-Assessment in Foreign Language Learning*:

LISTENING	
☐ I understand the language as well as a well-educated native.	5
☐	4.5
☐ I understand most of what is said in the language, even when said by native speakers, but have difficulty in understanding extreme dialect and slang. It is also difficult for me to understand speech in unfavourable conditions, for example through bad loudspeakers outdoors.	4
☐	3.5
☐ I can follow and understand the essential points concerning everyday and general things when spoken normally and clearly, but do not understand native speakers if they speak very quickly or use some slang or dialect.	3
☐	2.5
☐ I can follow and understand the essential points concerning everyday and general things when spoken slowly and clearly, but in the course of conversation I often have to ask for things to be repeated or made clearer. I only understand occasional words and phrases of statements made in unfavourable conditions, for example through loudspeakers outdoors.	2
☐	1.5
☐ I understand the meaning of simple requests, statements and questions if they are spoken slowly and clearly and if I have a chance of asking for them to be repeated. I only understand common words and phrases.	1
☐	0.5
☐ I do not understand the language at all.	0

Put a cross in the box which corresponds to your estimated level.

I understand practically everything that is said to me in English. → ☐ 10

☐ 9
☐ 8
☐ 7
☐ 6

LISTENING

☐ 5
☐ 4
☐ 3
☐ 2

I do not understand spoken English at all. → ☐ 1
☐ 0

Advantages
- Students take responsibility for their own level assessment. This is very much in tune with the whole philosophy of learner independence which lies behind self-access learning.
- Students are in the best position to know where their own strengths and weaknesses lie.
- In using self-assessment forms, students have the chance to assess themselves as being at different levels in different skills. Assessment can, therefore, be more sensitive.

Disadvantages
- Some students may not have the maturity to assess themselves honestly.
- Self-assessment forms may need to be translated into the student's first language.
- Asking students to assess themselves may come as a shock to students from some cultures. They may feel that professional assessment is part of what they are paying for.
- The kind of self-assessment outlined here is an absolute assessment in that it relates to performance in the real world. The point was made however, at the start of this section, that what is required is assessment related to the learning materials on offer. It may not be easy, therefore, to relate such an absolute assessment to an abstract notion of level in a study centre. Self-assessment may be more useful for purposes of needs analysis (see below).

4 Ongoing assessment

If students use a self-access system for more than, say, a couple of months, then thought should be given to reassessment from time to time to establish whether the student's level has changed. The same method can be used to reassess as was used for the initial assessment, i.e. if initial assessment has been by means of a placement test then the same or a similar test can be administered for reassessment. A policy decision needs to be taken concerning who decides on the timing of reassessment: the teacher, the institution, or the student. As an alternative to formal reassessment, it may be more appropriate for some students to move to a higher level when they feel ready.

Full and effective use

Having provided self-access facilities, orientated the students to the system, and helped them to establish their correct level, teachers may be tempted to feel that all that can be done has been done. Experience has shown, however, that this is not enough. Left to sink or swim in this way, most students will sink, that is to say they will not make use of the system or they will make only very limited use of it. Self-access learning is quite a revolutionary new concept for many people and most students will need guidance and training in the 'why?' and 'how?' of self-access learning. There are various ways in which this can be tackled.

1 Needs assessment

An initial needs assessment session with a teacher or counsellor is vital if students are to be able to proceed to the next stage of setting themselves useful and realistic targets. Needs assessment should be based upon such things as the student's purpose in studying English (which may be restricted to a particular topic or skill, e.g. a reading knowledge of the language), the student's strengths and weaknesses, his or her preferred learning style, his or her preferred strategies in relation to learning in general and language learning in particular, and so on. The answers to such questions can best be found by providing a questionnaire for students to complete. The questionnaire then forms a written record that can be referred to later, and it also provides a framework for the first counselling session. Below are two examples of simple, clear forms adapted from Ellis and Sinclair, *Learning to Learn English*.

2.2 What kind of learner are you?

CLASSIFICATION	**T.NA/1 = Training. Needs analysis/1**
LEVEL	**Lower intermediate upwards**
AGE	**Adolescent/adult**
ACTIVITY TYPE	**Study guide**
AIM	To help you find out more about your own learning style and what you need to concentrate on while you are learning English.
INSTRUCTIONS	Complete the questionnaire. Check your answers in the key, and find out more about your learning style.
QUESTIONNAIRE	

Tick (√) your answers to these questions:	Usually	Sometimes	Almost never	Don't know
1 Did/do you get good results in grammar tests?				
2 Do you have a good memory for new words?				
3 Do you hate making mistakes?				
4 In class, do you get irritated if mistakes are not corrected?				

Tick (√) your answers to these questions:	Usually	Sometimes	Almost never	Don't know
5 Is your pronunciation better when you read aloud than when you have a conversation?				
6 Do you wish you had more time to think before speaking?				
7 Did/do you enjoy being in a class?				
8 Do you find it difficult to pick up more than two or three words of a new language when you are on holiday abroad?				
9 Do you like to learn new grammar rules, words, etc. by heart?				

KEY

Your score
3 points for each 'usually'
2 points for each 'sometimes'
1 point for each 'almost never' or 'never'
0 points for each 'don't know'

Total score: points

Score: 23–27 points: analytic?
You feel it is very important to be accurate at all times. You are probably good at the sort of language learning where you need to think carefully about grammar, the meanings of words and their formation, your pronunciation, etc. This is very often the sort of language learning you do when you are in class or studying alone.

Generally, it seems that the more analytic you are, the better you are able to do this sort of language learning. However, you may be able to help yourself become an even more successful language learner. See the following tips.

You need to concentrate on improving your fluency by:
- trying to speak more by taking every opportunity you can to use the language. Try talking to English-speaking friends, tourists, etc. as often as possible
- not worrying too much about your mistakes, as you may be too concerned with being accurate. Trying to be correct all the time is hard work and can stop you from communicating well. However, making mistakes is an important part of the learning process, and after you have spoken, you can usually remember some of your mistakes. This is the time to make a note to yourself to do something about them
- depending on yourself, as outside the classroom you won't always have a dictionary or a teacher to help you. The people you speak to won't be listening for your mistakes, but for what you are trying to say, so have more confidence in yourself.

Score: 14–22 points: a mixture?

Perhaps you are lucky enough to be quite good at the type of learning described above, as well as at the type of learning described below. In fact, many people are a mixture, although you may find that you are closer to one type than the other.

You are fortunate because you may be in a better position to judge what type of learning is best for each situation, and then vary your strategy. This means that you have the potential to become an even more successful language learner. See the following tips.

You need to:

- analyse yourself because the more you know about yourself, the more easily you will be able to improve your language learning. Reading the comments for all the scores in this quiz should help you to decide what areas you need to concentrate on
- get the right balance by experimenting with different approaches to language learning activities. Try concentrating on either being fluent or being accurate. After a while, you will discover which approach works best for a certain activity. Ask your teacher if you need advice while you are learning.

Score: 9–13 points: relaxed?

You are probably good at 'picking up' languages without really making too much effort. You sometimes feel, however, that you should be learning more grammar rules, but you do not enjoy this and quickly lose interest. You like languages and enjoy communicating with people.

You have a positive attitude towards foreign languages, but you could probably become an even more successful language learner. See the following tips.

You need to:

- take time to learn by spending more time thinking about and practising things like grammar, pronunciation, etc. Try to organize a regular time for learning alone
- be self-critical by correcting yourself. You may not worry about making mistakes or even notice when you are making them. Try to become aware of the mistakes you make regularly and then make a conscious effort to do something about them.

Score: 0–8 points: not sure?

Your score does not mean that you are not a good language learner! It probably means that this is perhaps the first time you have ever thought about your feelings towards language learning. Maybe you are not yet fully aware of what you think and do when you are learning. To know more about how you learn can be very useful in helping you to become a more successful language learner. See the following tips.

You need to:

- think about yourself as a language learner more by asking yourself these questions when you find yourself in a class or self-access centre: 'What am I doing?', 'How am I learning?', 'Is it good?' You can train yourself to become more aware of your own learning habits and preferences
- ask for help because your teacher knows about learning and can help you analyse what you do. Use your teacher to find out about learning as you would use your dictionary to find out about words
- do this quiz again later on when you have had time to experience and think more about learning. You should find that you will know yourself better.

2.3 Needs analysis

CLASSIFICATION	**T.NA/2 = Training. Needs analysis/2**
LEVEL	**Lower intermediate upwards**
AGE	**Young adult/adult**
ACTIVITY TYPE	**Study guide**
AIM	To help you analyse your language needs and think about your long term language learning aims.
PREPARATION	1 Before you start your course, it is a good idea to think carefully about what you need or want English for. Start by thinking of either 'situations' or 'skills':

- *Situations*: you need to use English for, e.g. attending international conferences, going to the post office, etc.
- *Skills*: you need to have English for, e.g. listening/viewing, speaking, reading, writing.

2 Then, decide whether vocabulary or grammar (or both) are important in each situation or for each skill. You can then do your own needs analysis, like this:

Stig is a Swedish Youth Hostel warden. For his personal needs analysis he started with 'situations', then thought about the 'skills' he needed. He then decided whether for him vocabulary or grammar (or both) were important for each situation.

Needs analysis		Important?	
Situations	Skills	Vocabulary	Grammar
Youth Hostel Reception desk:			
– welcoming new guests	speaking	✓	
– giving Youth Hostel information	speaking	✓	
– explaining regulations	speaking	✓	✓
– answering enquiries	listening + speaking	✓	
– putting up notices	writing	✓	✓

INSTRUCTIONS   1 Now think about your own language needs and fill in the chart.

Needs analysis		Important?	
Situations	Skills	Vocabulary	Grammar

2 How much do you know/can you do already? Consider each area or skill and circle the number which you think is your level on a scale of 1 to 5:
1 = this is the standard I would like to reach — my goal.
5 = I can do very little. I am a long way from my goal.

Vocabulary	1	2	3	4	5
Grammar	1	2	3	4	5
Listening/viewing	1	2	3	4	5
Speaking	1	2	3	4	5
Reading	1	2	3	4	5
Writing	1	2	3	4	5

3 Number the six areas or skills according to how much priority (importance) you want to give them during this course, 1 = highest priority and 2 = lowest priority.

Skills/Areas	Priority Rating
Vocabulary	
Grammar	
Listening/viewing	
Speaking	
Reading	
Writing	

Comments to the teacher

The awareness-raising activities are adapted from G Ellis and B Sinclair, *Learning to Learn English.*

2 Setting targets

Students need to set themselves targets so that their work has a purpose. Most students will need help at least in the initial stages. Ideally, each student should have a tutor who will help him or her explore his or her language learning needs, and on the basis of the needs assessment process, set realistic targets. (The frequency of tutorials will be determined by institutional constraints.)

If they are to be taken seriously, learning targets have to be set down clearly on paper. Below are some suggestions for formats to help students.

2.4 Individual study plan

CLASSIFICATION   **T.TA/1 = Training. Targets/1**

LEVEL   **All**

AGE   **Adolescent/adult**

ACTIVITY TYPE   **Study guide**

AIM   To help you set yourself targets for your own study programme. Clear targets will help you make better use of your study time.

INSTRUCTIONS   Fill in your own study plan, following the format below.

STUDY PLAN

Date . . . .

Name . . . . Level . . . .

Number of hours a week I will spend on private study . . . .

The time of the day/week when I can best study is . . . .

Number of weeks this plan covers . . . .

In my private study I need to . . . .

. . . .

. . . .

The thing(s) I need to improve most is/are . . . .

. . . .

. . . .

My study timetable

Week no.	Subject	No. of hours	Activities planned

2.5 Individual contract

CLASSIFICATION	**T.TA/2 = Training. Targets/2**
LEVEL	**All**
AGE	**Adolescent/adult**
ACTIVITY TYPE	**Study guide**
AIM	To help you set yourself clear targets for your study programme so that you can make the best use of your private study time.
INSTRUCTIONS	Fill in your own study contract, following the format below.
CONTRACT	For the period beginning . . . . to . . . . . .

1 I will study on my own for at least . . . . . . hours a week.

2 I need to work on the following skills:

Reading ☐
Listening ☐
Writing ☐
Speaking ☐
Grammar ☐
Vocabulary ☐

3 Within the main areas ticked above I need to work particularly on:

Reading: . . . .
Listening: . . . .
Writing: . . . .
Speaking: . . . .
Grammar: . . . .
Vocabulary: . . . .

4 I will do at least . . . . . . activities a week in each of the sections I have ticked above.

5 I will arrange to meet my tutor at least . . . . times a week/month in order to discuss my progress.

Signed . . . . Witnessed . . . .

3 Pathways

Another way of helping students to make full and effective use of self-access facilities is to provide 'pathways' through the system. Pathways are ready-made mini study programmes which can take the form of flow-charts or just lists of suggested activities or activity types to be tackled in a certain order. It is perfectly possible to provide a number of pathways at different levels and for different skills areas or for different special purposes, so that students are provided with a choice of pathways.

The disadvantage of such pathways is that they take responsibility away from the student for setting his or her own goals. Artificial, 'off-the-peg' targets are offered, which may or may not fit the students' needs. Nevertheless, pathways do have their role to play in situations where students, because of their age, their culture, their lack of experience of independent learning, are just not capable of constructing a coherent study programme for themselves, even though they may be helped by a teacher to analyse their needs etc. Pathways are easy to use and they can act as interim measures, guiding students into constructing their own self-study programmes. They are like maps of what may be unknown territory. When students have managed to find their way with a map, then they can be abandoned with a compass and left to find their own way! Below is just one example of a pathway.

2.6 Reading programme

CLASSIFICATION **T.PA/1 = Training. Pathways/1**

LEVEL **Intermediate**

AGE **Junior/young adult**

ACTIVITY TYPE **Study guide**

FOCUS **Reading**

AIM To help you plan a programme of work for reading.

PROGRAMME **1** Work through at least one activity a day from the self-access Reading section. Look for activities with the classification R.CL/..., R.ST/..., R.CO/..., R.IT/... . (Make sure you vary your choice. Don't always work on the same kind of activity.)

2 Read at least one article a day from a current English language newspaper or magazine.
Or
Read at least one text a day from the Reading Laboratory and do the work card that goes with the text.

3 Choose an English book to read that interests you. Spend at least half an hour a day reading it. (Make a note of new useful vocabulary, if you wish, but don't use your dictionary too much.) When you've finished the book, write a review of it (see R.RE/1).

Comments to the teacher

1 Construct pathways with mixed skills work, around a common theme, if possible. (See 'Bridging the gap' in this chapter.)

2 Pathways can be built into self-access material. In this book many of the 'Preparation' and 'Follow-up' sections act as pathways (see 4.19 and 4.8 respectively). Study guides can also act as pathways (see 4.24).

4 Selling the product

If students are to make full use of self-access facilities, they first need to be sold on the necessity of assuming responsibility for their own learning and working on their own. Highflown educational ideals may well not carry much weight. Students must not get the impression that they are being used a guinea pigs in an educational experiment that fascinates the pedagogues but leaves them cold.

Probably the best advertisement for the system will be that it works for them; that they feel that the self-access learning they engage in is useful, and that they can make progress without being 'taught at'.

Conventional marketing techniques should not be spurned. How about bright signs and posters which change every couple of weeks highlighting some particular activity or area of the system and making it seem inviting? Display stands for new books and materials with the word 'New!' prominent are also a good idea. Areas and notice boards for the display of students' written work are also a good selling point, in that students get inspiration from one another.

Ongoing learner training in all aspects of private language study is essential if students are to continue to find self-access learning satisfying. An unobtrusive way of providing gradual learner training and development is to build study guides into the system concerning ways of improving speaking skills, vocabulary learning, the importance of good spelling, etc. There are several examples in this book of such study guides.

5 Monitoring and evaluation

Students should be encouraged to keep records of work they have done. This is best achieved by providing them with a standard record form which is very easy to devise and which they fill in. It is highly desirable that students have periodic access to a teacher or counsellor who can monitor their progress and discuss whether targets set are being achieved or whether there needs to be some reassessment of the learning programme for one reason or another. Such a counselling session can renew enthusiasm and set students off with fresh vigour in their quest for self-access learning.

6 Bridging the gap

In most institutions self-access facilities will exist alongside conventional classroom-based learning, and it is desirable to consider ways in which links can be forged between the two environments. Such links can serve the dual purpose of enriching classroom-based learning and familiarizing students with self-access facilities. Within a conventional teacher-directed language programme, the study centre or library can be a valuable resource for information-gathering tasks and for individualized language work encouraging students to look beyond the classroom. And once students have been directed to make use of the self-access and/or library facilities by teachers as part of a lesson or assignment, they are more inclined to return of their own volition because their confidence has been increased and their interest awakened.

There are doubtless many ways of bridging the gap between the classroom and the school's self-access or library facilities. A brief description of three of the possibilities is included here.

Theme-based pathways

Teachers often plan a series of lessons around a particular topic or theme. The theme may reflect the organization of the coursebook they are using, or they may be using their own materials and responding to the needs of their own students. One useful idea is to list, or incorporate into a flow-chart, self-access materials for listening, reading, vocabulary, etc, which exist in the self-access centre and which have the same theme or topic as is being treated in class. Students can then pursue such pathways on their own outside class. Alternatively, lessons can be scheduled to take place in the centre, during which each student chooses to work on what he or she feels is useful from the pathway, with the teacher on hand to give guidance where needed. (I heard this idea from Felicity O'Dell, a teacher at The Eurocentre, Cambridge.)

Investigative quizzes

One way of encouraging students to make good use of a study centre is to give them carefully constructed investigative quizzes from time to time. The questions in this kind of quiz are not intended to be answered on the spot from the students' existing pool of knowledge, but are rather intended to lead to investigation in the self-access centre, focusing on reference and information-gathering skills. Students can work individually or in groups, and if quizzes on a variety of topics are available, they can choose which quiz they wish to work on. Students might wish to construct a quiz themselves for others to work on, once they have experienced working on quizzes themselves. Here is an example of an investigative quiz constructed by Martyn Ford, a teacher at The Eurocentre, Brighton.

2.7 The arts in Britain

CLASSIFICATION	**T.BR/1 = Training. Bridging the gap/1**
LEVEL	**Advanced**
AGE	**Adolescent/adult**
ACTIVITY TYPE	**Quiz**
AIM	To familiarize you with sources of information available to you, and to give you practice in reference skills such as using indexes, contents lists, sub-headings, etc. To have fun!
QUIZ	**Background to Britain - an arts quiz**

1 What is the annual Booker Prize for?

2 Name two famous British orchestras.

3 At what time of the year can you see a pantomime? What type of story is used as the basis for a pantomime?

4 Sherlock Holmes is a famous fictional detective. Who invented him? What is the name of Holmes's assistant?

5 Who were the Pre-Raphaelites? To which period of history do they belong?

6 What are the Promenade Concerts? Where are they held, and at what time of year?

7 What kind of music can you hear at Ronnie Scott's club in London?

8 What sort of entertainments were composed by Gilbert and Sullivan? Give the title of one of these entertainments.

9 What is Poets' Corner, and where can you see it?

10 Which of the arts is Drury Lane in London particularly associated with?

11 J M Barrie wrote a famous children's story. What is it called?

12 In which two cities does the Royal Shakespeare Company have a permanent home?

13 Why is the Victoria and Albert Museum so called? Where exactly is it, and what is it especially famous for?

14 What is the Eisteddfod?

15 Edward Elgar and Ralph Vaughan Williams are famous in which branch of the arts?

16 Who or what is Winnie the Pooh?

17 At which London art gallery is there a collection of the paintings of J M W Turner?

18 What kind of entertainment would you see at Glyndebourne? Where is it?

19 Name two famous writers associated with the Bloomsbury Group.

20 Using the magazines *Radio Times* and *TV Times*, find the name

of one arts review programme on television, and one on radio.

21 What was Henry Moore famous for?

22 Give the address in London of the National Film Theatre.

23 Why do people sometimes take valuable works of art to Sotheby's and Christie's?

24 What was the Mersey Sound?

25 Give the name of the famous miser in Charles Dickens' story *A Christmas Carol*.

List of references

A Dictionary of Britain by Adrian Room.

Britain Today by Richard Musman

Concise Oxford Dictionary of English Literature

The Avenel Companion to English & American Literature

Theatre in Britain by Susan Holden

Spotlight on British Theatre by Jan King

For Queen & Country: Britain in the Victorian Age (Mirror of Britain series)

The Crack in the Teacup: Britain in the Twentieth Century (Mirror of Britain series)

The London Encyclopaedia

Comments to the teacher

1 If your institution does not possess a library or resource centre, you can construct a quiz based on a small number of reference books (as this one was) and take the relevant books into the classroom. Students will still be practising valuable reference and skimming and scanning skills.

2 Many different kinds of activity seem to fall under the heading of 'project work'. It can be a relatively minor affair involving the investigation of a limited area, or it can constitute the nucleus of a language learning programme (see G Carter and H Thomas 'Dear Brown Eyes – experiential learning in a project-oriented approach', *English Language Teaching Journal*, Vol. 40/3 (1986). Project work generally involves the gathering of information, both from reference sources such as libraries, and also from interviews with live informants. Once all the material on a particular topic of interest or concern has been amassed, the final presentation of information can take the form of a folder of work by an individual or group of individuals, a display of some kind, a video, etc. This could then be stored in the self-access centre, if appropriate, for other students to refer to.

Whatever form of project work is chosen, a resource centre will be an extremely useful asset, both in terms of information-gathering, and also in terms of self-access language work on areas that may have been identified as necessary for the successful completion of the project such as letter writing, making telephone calls, report writing, etc. (See *Project Work* by D L Fried-Booth in this series.)

3 Receptive skills

Introduction

The receptive skills of reading and listening are well-suited to self-access work. For one thing, it is easy to provide feedback to the students in the form of tapescripts, reading texts, and answers to comprehension questions. The students themselves can, to a large extent, provide their own feedback because they generally know if they have understood or not. Reading and listening texts also provide the students with data concerning language in use which can be consciously used by the students as a language model.

In addition, the receptive skills are ideal for self-access learning because they can supply students with comprehensible input, which is provided by a reading or listening text and which can be understood because of the context or because of personal experience, etc. even though the text itself may be at a level just slightly above what students can easily understand. From such input students may consciously or unconsciously acquire new language at the same time as they are focusing on another task connected with the text.

Reading

Of all the language skills, reading is the most necessary for independent learning, for through reading students can gain access to further knowledge, both about the language and about other subjects. Self-access tasks can be used to train students in intensive and extensive reading skills and they are a good way of introducing students to a world of reading beyond the classroom (see, for instance, the suggestions for further reading in 3.1, 3.2, and 3.3 below, and the ideas in the section on extensive reading later in this chapter).

Intensive reading – short texts

The first section concerns activities based on short reading texts where the emphasis is on careful, concentrated reading.

Cloze texts

Cloze texts are texts with words or phrases blanked out. They are easy to prepare and can be very useful in training the skill of anticipation in reading, i.e. the ability to make predictions about what may be coming next in a text. They also provide opportunities for focusing on features of the text such as cohesion and organization (see 3.1).

Scrambled texts

These activities are very simple to prepare and yet they are extremely useful in that students have to focus very carefully on relevant features of text organization (see 3.2).

Comprehension exercises

This type of reading exercise is far from new or unusual, yet it can provide useful feedback for students on their reading ability and level of comprehension. Fixed-response question types which have only one correct answer are the ones best suited for self-access, in particular multiple-choice and true/false questions (see 3.3).

Information transfer

Although comprehension questions are a useful pedagogical device, in real life students read not in order to answer questions but, among other things, to gain information from the text. One very good way of training students to do this effectively is to require them to transfer written information into some visual or tabular form (see 3.4).

Reading laboratories

Reading laboratories are collections of graded texts plus comprehension and language work at different levels. Keys are provided so that students can mark their own work and once they have completed a reasonable number of texts satisfactorily at one level they can move up to the next level – the original self-access package!

Reading laboratories are popular with students because they feel that their learning is somehow organized and they can see that they are making progress. Activity 3.5 is an example of an activity from a published reading laboratory.

3.1 Dangerous coconuts

CLASSIFICATION	R.CL/1 = Reading. Cloze exercise/1
LEVEL	Intermediate
AGE	Young adult/adult
ACTIVITY TYPE	Cloze text
AIM	To focus on textual cohesion and to practise reading prediction and reading comprehension skills.
PREPARATION	You may need to look up the following words in a dictionary if you do not already know what they mean: *a balcony, a coconut, a palm (tree), a thud, to linger, wealthy*.

INSTRUCTIONS

1 Read the passage below and find a word from the following list which will fit into each blank space:

because	should	there
but	skull	met
would	to	this
who	found	fruit
often	nut	and

Be careful! There are more words in the list than you need.

2 Write the answers on another piece of paper or in an exercise book. Do not write on this card.

My room in the hotel had a little balcony, and from (1) . . . I could step straight down on the beach. There were tall coconut palms growing all around, and every so (2) . . . an enormous green (3) . . . the size of a football would fall out of the sky (4) . . . drop with a thud on the sand. It was considered foolish (5) . . . linger underneath a coconut palm (6) . . . if one of those things landed on your head, it (7) . . . smash your (8) . . . . The Jamaican girl (9) . . . came in to tidy my room told me that a wealthy American called Mr Wasserman had (10) . . . his end in precisely (11) . . . manner only two months before.

From 'The boy who talked with animals' from *The Wonderful Story of Henry Sugar* by Roald Dahl.

KEY

1 there	5 to	9 who
2 often	6 because	10 met
3 nut	7 would	11 this
4 and	8 skull	

FOLLOW-UP 1

Read the rest of this story or read another story by Roald Dahl.

FOLLOW-UP 2

Do some more cloze texts. Look for activities with the same classification as this one (R.CL/) but with a different number on the end.

FOLLOW-UP 3

Find a partner, preferably another student who is at about the same level as you, who wants to practise reading. Copy out another text leaving some words blank. (Make sure the words can be guessed.) Ask your partner to try to fill in the missing words. He or she can then prepare a text for you in the same way.

Comments to the teacher

1 It is important to blank out only those words and phrases which native speakers would be able to predict, e.g. words relating to cohesive structure – in the example above numbers 1, 4, 6, 9, and 11; grammatical structure – numbers 5 and 7; lexical collocation and set phrases – numbers 3 and 10; or knowledge of the world – numbers 3 and 8. Words which should not be blanked out are content words such as *beach*, *football*, or *linger*, because if these were blanked out there would be more than one possible answer.

2 If you wish the students to focus on one specific area such as linking words, or other cohesive devices such as pronouns, then cloze texts can be prepared which have only these particular items blanked out.

3 To make the exercise harder, do not give your students a list of words to choose from. Make sure, however, that the words are predictable for native speakers.

3.2 Sleep

CLASSIFICATION	R.SC/1 = Reading. Scrambled text/1
LEVEL	Advanced
AGE	Adult
ACTIVITY TYPE	Scrambled text
TOPIC	Science/sleep
AIM	To encourage active reading comprehension and to focus on how a text is organized.
PREPARATION	There are one or two technical terms in the text that follows, but they are explained in the text, so do not worry.
INSTRUCTIONS	Put the following list of sentences in their correct order so that they form a short report. The opening sentence is indicated in italics. Write down the numbers of the sentences in their correct order on a separate sheet of paper. Do not write on this card.
TASK SHEET	1 When you dream, the activity in your brain can be measured by a machine called an electroencephalogram (EEG), which produces a pattern of waves.
	2 The other is known as quiet or non-REM sleep.
	3 *There are two kinds of sleep.*
	4 These waves are similar to those produced when you are awake.
	5 Altogether you spend about twenty per cent of each night in active sleep and it is during active sleep that you dream.
	6 One is known as active or rapid-eye-movement (REM) sleep, because your eyes move around even though they are closed.
	Adapted from *The Young Scientist Book of the Human Body* by Susan Meredith, Ann Goldman, and Tom Lissauer.
KEY	3, 6, 2, 5, 1, 4.

EXPLANATION　　If you had difficulty with this activity, notice how the text moves from known information to new information. Apart from the first sentence, new information is built on to what is already known. The known information usually comes at the beginning of the sentence and the new information at the end. Notice also that the use of *the* indicates something which has already been mentioned, that is to say *the* only appears under the 'known' column:

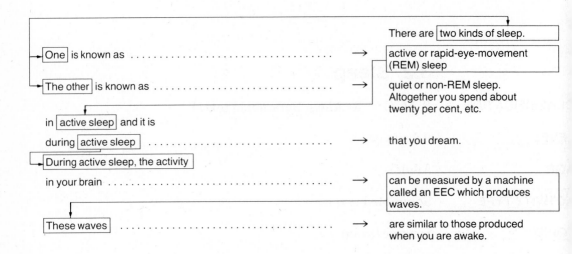

FOLLOW-UP 1　　If you are interested in scientific subjects in general, or in the language of science, try reading some longer texts on the subject: in the section on extensive reading (later in this chapter) look for texts with the topic 'science'.

FOLLOW-UP 2　　Find a text which you feel is the right level for you, i.e. not too easy, and not too difficult. Ask a friend to choose a paragraph from the text and to copy out the sentences in the wrong order. Then you try to put them in the correct order.

Comments to the teacher

1 To prepare scrambled texts, select a paragraph of text, type out the sentences in random order, and give each sentence a number. Unsimplified authentic texts may be used as in the example or, for lower levels, choose simplified texts from Readers and other EFL materials.

2 As a variation, choose a longer text and put the paragraphs in the wrong order, and number them. Ask the students to arrange them in the correct order.

3 Another alternative would be to extract key sentences from a longer text. Mix them up so that they are not in the order they occur in the text, and then put them at the end of the text. Ask the students to decide where there is a sentence missing in the text and which sentence fits in each case.

3.3 Introducing Sherlock Holmes

CLASSIFICATION   **R.CO/1 = Reading. Comprehension activity/1**

LEVEL   **Lower intermediate**

AGE   **Adolescent/young adult**

ACTIVITY TYPE   **Comprehension activity**

AIM   To read and look closely at the most important parts of the text and to check comprehension.

PREPARATION   Look up the following words in a dictionary if you don't know them: *a wound, to heal, a client.*

INSTRUCTIONS   Read the text below and say whether the sentences which follow are true or false.

TASK SHEET

For many years, I shared an apartment in London with my friend, Sherlock Holmes,

My name is Doctor Watson. I worked as a doctor in the British Army for several years. While I was in the army, I
5   travelled to many strange and interesting places. I had   5
many exciting adventures.

Then one day, in Afghanistan, I was shot in the shoulder. My wound was deep and took many months to heal. I nearly died from pain and fever. At last I got better, but I
10 could not work in the army any more. I retired from the   10
army and came back to England.

That is why I was living in London with Sherlock Holmes. I had known my friend for many years. Our address was 221B, Baker Street, in the centre of the city.
15   I enjoyed sharing an apartment with Holmes. My friend   15
was a very clever man. He was the most famous private detective in London. He helped to solve crimes and catch criminals.

When people were in trouble or needed help, they came
20 to Holmes. Sometimes the police came to Holmes and   20
asked for help in catching a criminal.

Sherlock Holmes did not care if his clients were rich or poor. He enjoyed solving their interesting problems. He was very happy when he was working. It was the most
25 important thing in his life.   25

From *The Sign of Four* by Sir Arthur Conan Doyle, retold by Anne Collins.

True or false?

1 Sherlock Holmes and Doctor Watson lived in the same place.

2 Doctor Watson was a soldier in the army.

3 Doctor Watson came back to England because he was tired of the army.

4 When Doctor Watson came back to England, he got to know Sherlock Holmes.

5 Sherlock Holmes was a detective in the police force.

6 Sherlock Holmes helped people in trouble whether they could pay or not.

7 Sherlock Holmes liked using his mind.

KEY

1 True (lines 1/2 and lines 13/14).

2 False. He was a doctor in the army (lines 3/4).

3 False. He 'retired from' (= 'left') the army and came back to England because he could not work. He could not work because he had been very ill (lines 7/11).

4 False. He knew Holmes before he went to Afghanistan (line 13).

5 False. Sherlock Holmes was a private detective. He sometimes helped the police but he did not work for them as an employee (lines 16/17 and 20/21).

6 True (lines 22/23).

7 True (lines 23/25).

FOLLOW-UP 1

If you got fewer than 4 answers right, try a comprehension exercise at elementary level.

If you got between 4 and 6 answers right, try some more comprehension exercises at this level.

If you got all the answers right, try a comprehension exercise at intermediate level.

FOLLOW-UP 2

If you are interested in Sherlock Holmes, read the rest of the story.

Comments to the teacher

1 Students can gain more from such activities if the relevant line reference to the text is given after each answer.

2 Note that students can be advised to move to a lower or higher level depending on how many answers they got right. This technique can be used with many other activities.

3 Many published Readers contain examples of this kind of activity which it is possible to adapt for self-access.

3.4 Superman versus smoking

CLASSIFICATION   R.IT/1 = Reading. Information transfer/1

LEVEL   Intermediate

AGE   Adolescent/young adult

ACTIVITY TYPE   Information transfer

AIM   To extract and recognize relevant information from a reading text.

PREPARATION   Think about the problem of children smoking. How can they be persuaded not to start? Do you think the problem is a serious one? Make a list of three ways in which children could be prevented from trying cigarettes.

INSTRUCTIONS   Read the following text and use the information to complete the questionnaire below. Write the information on a separate piece of paper. Do not write on this card.

TASK SHEET

NOW I NEED YOUR HELP KIDS. IN MY LIFE LONG CAMPAIGN AGAINST THE DREADED NICK O' TEEN. NEVER SAY YES TO A CIGARETTE.

Over 100,000 primary school children wrote supporting Superman in his fight against smoking during the first four weeks of the Health Education Council's recent £500,000 campaign.

The campaign, which began just after Christmas, uses the Superman character to persuade 7- to 11-year-olds that they should 'crush the evil Nick O'Teen' and never say yes to a cigarette.

Most of the budget has been spent on producing and showing a cartoon television commercial, which features Superman in conflict with the arch-enemy Nick O'Teen.

The campaign, which is seen as a long-term project, is based on careful research. This showed that one in three adult smokers started before they were nine and that 80 per cent of children who smoke regularly grow up to be smokers. For boys, the average age for starting to smoke was found to be 9.7 years while for girls, it was 11.2 years.

QUESTIONNAIRE

Country __Britain_____	Intended public (age, sex . . .) _____
Budget _____	Media used – television ☐
	– radio ☐
Opening date _____	– posters ☐
	– magazines/comics/
Closing date _____	newspapers ☐
	– other ☐
	Slogans _____
Estimated success – high ☐	
– average ☐	
– low ☐	

KEY

Country __Britain_____	Intended public (age, sex . . .) boys + girls aged 7–11
Budget £500,000 ____	Media used – television ☑
	– radio ☐
Opening date December_	– posters ☐
Closing date ? 'long term'	– magazines/comics/
	newspapers ☑
	– other ☐
	Slogans 'Crush the evil Nick O Teen',
	'Never say yes to a cigarette
Estimated success – high ☑ (over 100,000 children wrote)	
– average ☐	
– low ☐	

Comments to the teacher

1 Almost any informative text and some fictional ones can be reorganized in this way. Look carefully at the information contained in the text and sort the information into categories which can then be represented in schematic, tabular form.

2 As a variation, students can use the information contained in a text to draw or complete a diagram, a chart, a map, a plan, etc.

3.5 Weekend

CLASSIFICATION	**R.RL/1 = Reading. Reading laboratory/1**
LEVEL	**Elementary**
AGE	**Adult**
ACTIVITY TYPE	**Reading laboratory**
AIM	To practise reading and understanding real texts.
PREPARATION	Look at the text below but do not read the words. What kind of text is it? Where would you see it?

Read the text and write down the missing words on a separate piece of paper. There are ten missing words.

From *Reading Choices* by David Jolly.

This is an advertisement. You could find it in any family magazine. It is advertising sweets. The ten missing words are: *family, up, down, holiday, pounds, francs, kitchen sink, half past eight, Paris, Weekend.*

Comments to the teacher

1 Published reading laboratories are available: SRA publish a variety of reading laboratories for adults, children, college students, and ESL students. One published specifically for EFL is *Reading Choices* by David Jolly, from which the above example is taken. The laboratories are self-contained, and all the instructions, level codings, and tasks are kept in one box.

2 *Making your own reading lab*: published reading laboratories are obviously extremely useful in that you have an instant bank of self-access materials at varying levels. They are, however, extremely expensive and if there are not enough resources available to purchase a published reading laboratory, or your students have specialist needs not covered by existing published material, then it is perfectly possible to create one's own scheme.

In order to assemble a homemade reading laboratory, you first need to collect a large number of interesting and varied texts. Examples of possible sources for such texts include: newspaper and magazine articles, cookery books, advertisements, extracts from novels and short stories, extracts from plays, informative leaflets, extracts from encyclopaedias and non-fiction books, especially travel books and biographies, extracts from simplified Readers, and other published EFL material containing simple texts, etc. If appropriate for your students, then texts with a particular ESP or EAP bias can be used. In any case, the beauty of making your own scheme is that you can base it very firmly on the interests and concerns of *your* students. You can encourage the students themselves to contribute texts. Students can be particularly helpful in suggesting sources for EAP and ESP-type texts where the teacher may not be particularly expert. Once you have collected your texts, sort them into levels. Four or five levels is probably enough to begin with, for every twenty-five students who will use the scheme (presuming mixed levels), you should aim to have at least ten to fifteen texts at each level at the start, and this number can gradually be increased. Write fixed-response comprehension questions (see 3.3) for each text and supply a key which can go on the reverse side of the card. The texts and questions themselves are best stuck onto card of a uniform size and then laminated or covered in self-seal clear film. Mark all the cards clearly with their level, colour coding is probably the best way. Give each card a uniquely identifying classification code which can just be a number (so that you get, say, blue 1, 2, 3, 4, etc., red 1, 2, 3, 4, etc.) and store them in a box with dividers between the different levels.

Level assessment: in order to assist students to find the level which is right for them, select a text in the middle of your range of difficulty and make it into a cloze test (see 3.1). Take a reasonable score on this test – say, sixty to seventy per cent – as your bench-mark for the middle level and then decide on the upper and lower level parameters in relation to this. This cloze test, together with a guide to the interpretation of scores, can then be used by all students as an entry test into the scheme. This will give you a rough guide to begin with but you will probably need to modify your system in the light of experience.

Progress: record sheets such as the one below can be supplied to students so that they can record each reading activity they do, note down how they performed, and get an overview of how they are progressing through the reading scheme.

Reading laboratory record sheet

Name . . . .

Colour	No.	Score	Comments

Extensive reading – longer texts

In addition to intensive reading of fairly short texts students need to read extensively and widely both for information and pleasure. Extensive reading of longer texts will increase their vocabulary and improve their general 'feeling' for the language.

Above a certain language level – intermediate or upper-intermediate – there is no reason why all the texts provided in this section should not be authentic, taken from brochures, leaflets, newspapers, magazines, reference books, and works of fiction, etc. These texts should be classified in terms of 'Topic' and 'Text-type', as well as by the usual categories of 'Level', 'Age', etc. And in order that students can select reading texts by topic or by text-type, there needs to be a topic index and a text-type index available (see Appendix 1 for sample topic and text-type classification systems).

Extensive reading should be regarded very much as an end in itself rather than always as a prerequisite for the delivery of an end-product, unless, that is, the students themselves wish to produce something. In this regard, extensive reading can be seen as self-directed learning in a broader and more independent sense than the fairly closely 'controlled' self-access tasks in the preceding section. For this reason, the activity which follows should not be imposed but only offered to those students who find it helpful.

3.6 Book review

CLASSIFICATION   **R.RE/1 = Reading. Review writing/1**

LEVEL   **Intermediate**

AGE   **Young adult/adult**

ACTIVITY TYPE   **Reading and review writing**

AIM   To encourage reflection on what has been read and to provide a record of reading achieved. To practise evaluative writing.

PREPARATION   Read a novel or short story that interests you.

INSTRUCTIONS   Use the review sheet below as a guide to writing a review of what you have read. For each novel or short story you read, complete one of these review sheets so that you build up a record of what you have read in English.

REVIEW SHEET   Title: . . . .
                      Author: . . . .
                      Publisher: . . . .
                      Category: (tick one)
                      Romance ☐   Historical   ☐
                      Horror   ☐   Science fiction   ☐
                      Crime   ☐   Other (describe) ☐
                      Spy   ☐
                      The most important characters: . . . .
                      . . . .
                      . . . .
                      Summary of the story: . . . .
                      . . . .
                      . . . .
                      What I liked: . . . .
                      . . . .
                      . . . .
                      What I disliked: . . . .
                      . . . .
                      . . . .
                      I do/do not recommend this book: . . . .
                      . . . .
                      . . . .

FOLLOW-UP   File your review alphabetically by the title of the book in the 'review file' so that other students can read it. Look at other reviews in the file. You may find a review of a book you would like to read.

Comments to the teacher

1 This is an example of a standard reading task, i.e. a task which can be applied to many different texts within a particular genre, in this case, a novel or short story. Standard review sheets like this save a lot of work for materials writers and allow new texts supplied by teachers and students to be added to the system with great ease. Try writing standard reading tasks for other genres such as newspaper leader articles, advertisements, letters, magazine articles, poems, etc. (see also 3.18).

2 If your institution has a study centre which includes a library then the books are to hand. If this is not the case, then consider starting a small class library. Access to a good variety and reasonably large number of books is vital to any extensive reading programme.

3 As a variation on the main activity for more advanced students, rewrite the review sheet to include 'Characterization', 'Style', etc. and replace the 'What I liked' and 'What I disliked' sections with a more open-ended 'Comments' section.

Listening

Listening lends itself to self-access in the same way that reading does. It is quite easy to produce questions and activities which have only one correct answer, and which are, therefore, easily marked. The section on intensive listening below has a number of examples of this type of activity. Listening in the real world, however, is obviously more complex and so while intensive practice of short duration helps build up confidence and skills in certain areas, there is also a need to provide the opportunity for more extensive and less controlled listening, and this will be dealt with in the section on longer texts later in this chapter.

Intensive listening – short texts

Minimal pairs
Minimal pairs activities provide practice in aural discrimination between individual sounds. They are closely linked with pronunciation practice, as the ability to recognize and correctly identify sound contrasts, is generally held to precede, or at least to be closely linked with, the ability to produce them appropriately (see 3.7).

Dictation
In its basic form, a dictation is quite simply a spoken or, for self-access, recorded text which the student has to reproduce in written form. Dictation is in many ways the perfect self-access activity since, from the teacher's point of view, it is extremely easy to prepare, and from the student's point of view, it is a demanding

task but one which gives the student precise and unambiguous feedback on his or her own performance.

But is dictation a useful, as well as convenient, self-access activity? Undoubtedly it does have a place in the development of accuracy in listening and writing skills. It is valuable for the student to be able to focus in a detailed way on the correspondence between sounds and their written forms, and more broadly, the student needs to employ all the knowledge he or she has concerning the structure of the language as an aid to interpretation. Dictation is far from being a mechanical activity and students often have to use a good deal of deduction to help them recreate the message they hear (see 3.8).

Listening cloze texts
Listening cloze activities are similar to reading cloze activities in that certain words in the transcript of a recorded text or dialogue are blanked out and students have to listen and fill in the blanks from what they hear. This kind of activity is good for focusing on particular items or areas of vocabulary, and it is also useful for elementary students who may find normal dictation too difficult (see 3.9).

Scrambled pictures
In this activity students arrange a number of pictures so as to reflect a story or sequence they have heard. The pictures, together with knowledge of the world, provide valuable support in helping students with a low level of English to understand what they hear (see 3.10).

Picture matching
Another possibility for exploiting a series or number of pictures is to ask students to decide which picture matches the spoken description they hear (see 3.11).

Texts with comprehension tasks
As with reading, the most obvious and traditional form of listening practice is to provide a listening text and set some kind of comprehension task on it (see 3.12).

Information transfer
Information transfer activities for listening practice involve the transfer of spoken information into a more visual form. Students can listen to a dialogue, a short talk, an announcement of some kind, a set of instructions, etc. and then, using the information obtained, they draw or complete a diagram, a family tree, a map, a plan, etc., or they fill in a chart or a table of some kind (see 3.13).

3.7 Helen and Ellen

CLASSIFICATION	**L.MP/1 = Listening. Minimal pairs/1**
LEVEL	**Intermediate to Advanced**
AGE	**Adolescent/adult**
LANGUAGE GROUP	**Useful for French speakers**
ACTIVITY TYPE	**Minimal pairs activity**
AIM	To practise hearing the difference between words beginning with /h/ and words which begin with a vowel.
PREPARATION	Look up the following words in a dictionary if you do not know them: *hearty, arty, heir, harbour, arbour*.
INSTRUCTIONS	On a separate piece of paper write down the letters of the pictures you hear described, in the order in which you hear them.
TASK SHEET	

Ellen

A. Ellen is hearty

C. Ellen heats up the pie

E. Ellen looks after her heir

G. Ellen and Hannah like harbours

Helen

B. Helen is arty

D. Helen eats up the pie

F. Helen looks after her hair

H. Helen and Anna like arbours

KEY	1C, 2F, 3B, 4D, 5G, 6A, 7E, 8H.
TAPESCRIPT	1 Ellen heats up the pie. 2 Helen looks after her hair. 3 Helen is arty. 4 Helen eats up the pie. 5 Ellen and Hannah like harbours. 6 Ellen is hearty. 7 Ellen looks after her heir. 8 Helen and Anna like arbours.
FOLLOW-UP	Try this activity again with a friend. Take it in turns to read the sentences while the other person tries to hear which picture each sentence goes with.

Comments to the teacher

1 Minimal pairs activities can use single words, as in *glass/grass*, or the words can be embedded in a sentence, in which case care needs to be taken that the context is equally feasible for both words, so that *Cows eat a lot of glass/grass* is obviously not satisfactory, whereas *There are many different varieties of glass/grass* is. (For examples of contextualized minimal pairs see *English Pronunciation Illustrated* by John Trim, from which the example is adapted, McLean *Start Listening,* Baker *Tree or Three?,* and Baker *Ship or Sheep?*)

2 It is a good idea to sort and store the practice material for different phonemic contrasts separately (i.e. to cut up the book and store the various sound contrasts separately), so that students have very precise access to the minimal pairs activities which are a problem for them. An information sheet to act as an overall guide for different nationalities would be useful. It could offer advice to the various first language groups, so that Japanese students for example, would be advised to use the /l/ versus /r/ pack, amongst others. (For information concerning the difficulties of different language groups see *Learner English* by Michael Swan and B Smith (1987).)

3.8 The seaside

CLASSIFICATION	L.DI/1 = Listening. Dictation/1
LEVEL	Intermediate
AGE	Young adult
ACTIVITY TYPE	Dictation

AIM	Detailed listening practice concentrating on accuracy in listening and writing.
INSTRUCTIONS	1 First, you will hear the text read without pauses. Do not write anything yet. Just listen. 2 You will now hear the text read with pauses. Write down what you hear on a separate piece of paper. Each short section will be repeated once. 3 Finally, you will hear the text read again without pauses. Read through and check what you have written.
KEY/TAPESCRIPT	In Britain, you are never very far from the coast and there are lots of seaside towns, called resorts, all round the country where people go for their holiday or just on a day trip. Brighton, on the south coast, is a famous seaside resort. There are entertainments of all kinds. Brighton Pier is a popular place to spend a few hours, especially if the weather is not good enough to stay on the beach. From *Spotlight on Britain* by S Sheerin, J Seath and G White.
FOLLOW-UP 1	If you found this dictation difficult, or if you made a lot of mistakes, study the tapescript carefully noticing all your mistakes. In one week's time, do this dictation again and see whether you can reduce the number of your mistakes.
FOLLOW-UP 2	If you found this dictation easy and you did not make many mistakes, try a dictation at the next level up. You can also make your own dictation: find a recording or make your own recording of a talk on a subject which interests you. Now try to write down a small part of the talk word for word, stopping the tape recorder as and when you need to.

Comments to the teacher

1 As a language learning activity, dictation has been out of favour for a number of years now, although just recently it seems to be regaining popularity. Dictation can be of great value for students studying on their own, particularly in a language like English where there appears to be so little systematic correspondence between phonological and orthographic forms.

Dictations are extremely easy to prepare, all that is needed is for native-speakers or near-native-speakers to record texts onto cassette and for students to be provided with those texts for the purpose of self-correction.

2 The learning potential of dictation can be increased and the testing factor decreased if students study a text before attempting it. They could also try the dictation again in a week's time if they

made more than a certain number of errors. These variations of procedure can either be incorporated into the rubric or the 'Follow-up' section of each individual dictation (see above) or students can be directed to an advice sheet on different approaches to dictation and the choice be left to them.

3 Another variation in dictation procedure is to insert no pauses when recording and let students use the 'pause' button on the tape recorder themselves as and when they need it (see 'Follow-up 2' above).

3.9 The Nuthatch

CLASSIFICATION   L.CL/1 = Listening. Cloze text/1

LEVEL   Intermediate

AGE   Adolescent/adult

ACTIVITY TYPE   Cloze text

TOPIC   Science/animals/birds

AIM   To practise listening for detail and to recall or learn specific items of vocabulary.

PREPARATION   You are going to hear a factual account of the habits of a bird called the 'Nuthatch'. You may need to look up the word *feat* before you start.

INSTRUCTIONS   Listen and fill in the blanks. Write your answers on a separate piece of paper.

TASK SHEET   If you ever see a bird walking down the (1) . . . of a tree head downwards, then you know that the bird must be a Nuthatch. Nuthatches are the only birds which perform this (2) . . . feat. They are quite small birds, about the size of a sparrow, and they have a very noticeable black (3) . . . running in a straight line from the beak, round the (4) . . . and beyond, to the back of the head. They live in (5) . . . trees throughout Europe and they feed on small insects, nuts, and (6) . . . .

KEY   1 trunk   2 acrobatic   3 stripe   4 eye   5 pine   6 seeds

Comments to the teacher

1 In a reading cloze activity the words that are blanked out have to be predictable because students are supplying the missing words from inside their own heads. In a listening cloze activity, however, the words that are blanked out need not be the predictable words but rather can be the unpredictable ones, so that students really do have to listen.

2 When preparing a listening cloze activity the gaps should not come too close together. There probably needs to be a minimum of something like ten to fifteen words between gaps, depending to a certain extent on the students' level.

3 As a variation on the example above, and in order to focus specifically on the presence of weak forms and contractions in normal spoken English, function words such as auxiliary verbs, prepositions, pronouns, etc. can be blanked out and students asked to state how many words are missing in the case of each blank.

4 Another variation of the listening cloze is to blank out some of the words of a song (preferably a pop song in the case of teenagers). This activity tends to be extremely popular!

3.10 A busy life

CLASSIFICATION	**L.SP/1 = Listening. Scrambled pictures/1**
LEVEL	**Elementary**
AGE	**Junior/adolescent**
ACTIVITY TYPE	**Listening and sorting scrambled pictures**
AIM	To listen to and understand a story.
PREPARATION	You are going to hear a short story about a day in the life of a cat called Tabitha. Have you got a pet? Before you listen, think about its day and the kind of things it might do.
INSTRUCTIONS	**1** Write down the numbers 1 to 6 on a separate piece of paper. Listen to the story. Write down the letter of the first picture you hear described next to number 1. Do the same for numbers 2 to 6. You will hear the story twice.
	2 Check your answers with the key when you have finished the activity.

TASK SHEET

KEY

1C, 2D, 3F, 4B, 5A, 6E.

TAPESCRIPT

Early every morning Tabitha has some food and then goes for a long walk. Sometimes she catches a mouse in the field. She likes climbing trees and watching the birds. When she is in the garden, she often sits on the fence and watches the cat next door. Sometimes, when she is thirsty, she has a drink from the garden pond. When the weather is cold, Tabitha enjoys lying in front of a big fire.

Comments to the teacher

Strip cartoons in newspapers and magazines are valuable sources of ideas for scrambled picture activities, as are leaflets and diagrams indicating stages in a process. Be careful not to use pictures where the correct sequence can be deduced from knowledge of the world without even having to listen.

3.11 The big fight

CLASSIFICATION

L.PM/1 = Listening. Picture matching/1

LEVEL

Lower intermediate

AGE

Adolescent/adult

ACTIVITY TYPE

Picture matching

AIM

To listen to and understand a description of a scene.

You are going to hear a description of a scene. There is a man, a woman, and a television set in the scene. If you do not already know it, look up the meaning of *clenched fist* in the dictionary, before you start.

INSTRUCTIONS   Listen and decide which picture in the story is being talked about: A, B, C, D, or E. Write your answer on a separate piece of paper. Do not write on this card.

ASK SHEET

a

b

c

d

e

EY   Picture D is the picture being described.

APESCRIPT   There is a man and a woman in the picture and neither of them look happy. The man has his fists clenched and is standing up with one arm raised above his head. The woman has her hands over her eyes. There is a television in the room and there seems to be something wrong with it because we can see wavy lines on the screen.

Comments to the teacher

1 The more similar the pictures, the more difficult this activity becomes.

2 In preparing this activity, try to lead the listener into gradually eliminating pictures but withhold the final piece of information that will enable the students to positively identify which picture is being talked about until the last sentence, as in the example above.

3.12 Horoscope

CLASSIFICATION
L.CO/1 = Listening. Comprehension task/1

LEVEL
Upper intermediate

AGE
Young adult/adult

ACTIVITY TYPE
Listening text with comprehension task

AIM
To practise listening for specific information.

PREPARATION
You have 'dialled a horoscope' over the telephone and you are now about to hear today's horoscope. Copy the chart below onto a separate piece of paper. You do not need to know the dates of the star signs. You will hear them as you listen. Before you start listening read the 'advice'.

INSTRUCTIONS
As you listen, write in your chart the star signs of your three friends, and the number of the piece of advice which applies to each of them (one item only per person). Listen more than once, if necessary.

TASK SHEET
Advice
1 Start thinking more seriously about your job.
2 Do not spend so much money.
3 Do not be thoughtless with those around you.
4 Stay in tonight.
5 Do not do anything silly just because someone says nice things about you.
6 Do not quarrel with someone you love.

	Birth dates	Star sign	Advice (item no.)
Friend 1	12 November		
Friend 2	2 June		
Friend 3	6 August		

KEY

	Birth dates	Star sign	Advice (item no.)
Friend 1	12 November	Scorpio	1
Friend 2	2 June	Gemini	5
Friend 3	6 August	Leo	3

TAPESCRIPT

This is your telephone horoscope for today:

Aquarius (21 January – 19 February)
If you are going out this evening, make sure it is to a place you know well.

Pisces (20 February – 20 March)
If there are certain matters you have been worrying about recently, this is a good moment to share them with a friend or lover.

Aries (21 March – 20 April)
Avoiding trouble will not be easy today, especially if you let yourself get caught up in an argument with a loved one.

Taurus (21 April – 21 May)
The chances are you will come up with a clever idea to save money today. Congratulations!

Gemini (22 May – 21 June)
Do not let compliments or flattery from friends make you do something silly which you may regret later on.

Cancer (22 June – 23 July)
Lots of new friends may be coming into your life, and a lot of money going out if you do not start saving a bit more. Hold on to those purse strings.

Leo (24 July – 23 August)
Resist the temptation to act thoughtlessly towards friends and family. You will hurt them more than you realize.

Virgo (24 August – 23 September)
Do not get into a panic about work or money. You will only make yourself miserable. A night in will prove very relaxing.

Libra (24 September – 23 October)
Your romantic life may seem rather dull. If so, a change is in view.

Scorpio (24 October – 22 November)
If you have a job you may decide it is time to take it a lot more seriously. It could well lead to some quick promotion.

Sagittarius (23 November – 21 December)
A good time to go into business with a friend.

Capricorn (22 December – 20 January)
You will be feeling pretty confident just now. That makes it a good day to tackle anything difficult or unusual.

That is the end of today's horoscope.

Comments to the teacher

With listening comprehension it is extremely important to set the scene before the students listen. It is vital to give the students something approaching the contextual information that they would have in real life: who the speaker(s) is/are; who is being addressed; what the topic is; where the communication is taking place, and what its purpose is, etc. This contextualization can be provided by a short written paragraph or can be wholly or partially fulfilled with a picture of the speaker and/or the setting, etc.

3.13 Philip's party

CLASSIFICATION L.IT/1 = Listening. Information transfer/1

LEVEL Lower intermediate

AGE Adolescent/young adult

ACTIVITY TYPE Information transfer – spoken word to visual representation

AIM To practise listening for specific information concerning location.

PREPARATION It is Philip's birthday party and he has invited some friends to have a meal with him. You are going to hear where his guests are sitting around the table. Who is sitting where exactly?

INSTRUCTIONS 1 Before you start, copy the seating plan onto a separate piece of paper. Do not write on this card.
2 Listen carefully and fill in the names of the people in their correct places around the table on the plan.

TASK SHEET

It is Philip's birthday party today and so he is sitting at the head of the table. On his right sits his best friend James, who is sitting next to Mary, his girlfriend. Opposite Mary sits Robert with Sylvia on his right, and Anne on his left. Paul is sitting opposite Philip and is deep in conversation with Richard.

Comments to the teacher

1 Remember that if the activity involves filling something in or completing a drawing, etc. it will either be necessary to provide photocopies for students to work on or to make the basic visual simple enough to be easily copied, as in the example above. If you intend the students to copy the visual, do not forget to include instructions to this effect.

2 Another popular form of this kind of information transfer activity is picture dictation, in which students draw or complete a picture in accordance with what they hear. A more adult form of picture dictation can be based on combinations of geometric shapes.

3 Other ideas for listening tasks based on the principle of the reorganization of information can be found in Blundell and Stokes *Task Listening*, Ur *Teaching Listening Comprehension*, and for children, Scott *Are You Listening?*

Extensive listening – longer texts

In addition to the kind of intensive practice provided by activities like those included in the previous section, there is also a need among intermediate and advanced students for the opportunity to practise more extended listening. This opportunity represents a bridge for students between controlled listening, where texts are short and carefully selected or simplified, and autonomous listening in the real world. It is also a bridge between activities whose purpose is primarily pedagogical requiring very limited, clear-cut responses from students which are either 'right' or 'wrong', and the many varied responses to listening which occur in the real world.

The kinds of texts best suited to form this 'bridge' between controlled and autonomous listening are the sorts of texts which students themselves might choose to listen to, i.e. they should be interesting and informative or stimulate the imagination. The optimum length is probably somewhere between five and twenty minutes, so that students can start off with fairly short texts and gradually progress to longer ones. Material accompanying the texts needs to provide support for students, while allowing for a flexibility and variety of approaches and responses from individual students. There are a number of different ways in which this can be done.

As with the extensive reading section, authentic listening texts should be used as much as possible, especially for the higher level students (for advice on how to provide authentic material see the section on 'Sources for extensive listening material' later in this chapter). In addition, all items in this section should be classified according to topic and text-type, and access by topic and/or text-type should be possible for students (see Appendices 1 and 2).

Using tapescripts

Tapescripts are extremely valuable to students for a number of reasons: the mere presence of a tapescript encourages students to listen to what they might otherwise consider beyond them, and also provides them with the written form of words which they may not know, thereby enabling them to look up the words in a dictionary. A tapescript allows students to make detailed comparisons between the sounds of English and their written forms. For these reasons as many tapes as possible should be accompanied by tapescripts. Students can use tapescripts in a number of ways. Prepare a general study guide to using tapescripts like the one below, rather than repeating the instructions with each listening tape (see 3.14).

Summaries

Summaries of taped material can be useful for pragmatic reasons in that they are quicker to prepare than full tapescripts and yet, if they are detailed enough, they can still perform the functions of building confidence and aiding comprehension outlined above. What a summary will not provide is the opportunity to study the text and its phonology in detail.

Summaries, like tapescripts, can be used by students in a variety of ways, and a study guide similar to the one above for tapescripts can be prepared (see 3.15).

Comprehension questions

In preparing materials to accompany extended listening there is no need to feel that students always have to answer questions or demonstrate comprehension in some other way. Do not forget that extended listening is intended to be a bridge to autonomous listening and it is, therefore, appropriate to trust students to listen for pleasure or for interest or information without always requiring answers to activities. However, no doubt teachers and students will feel that at least some of the longer listening texts should be accompanied by comprehension questions, and these too can be used by the students in different ways. Once again, a general study guide can make this clear to students (see 3.16).

Reactive listening

Where the primary purpose of the speaker(s) is to interact rather than to inform, it is not a good idea to set comprehension questions of the type appropriate for factual content. It is far more appropriate to ask questions which focus on the speakers themselves, on their relationship to one another, and on the listener's reactions to what he or she hears.

Reactions can be very subjective and it is important to recognize that there cannot be any 'right' or 'wrong' answers as such with this activity. For this reason, it is more advisable to provide a 'Commentary' for students to consult, rather than a 'Key'.

Below is a prototype showing the kinds of questions that can be asked. The exact content and nature of the questions will, of course, depend on the text concerned (see 3.17).

Reading fiction onto tape

One of the most enjoyable listening experiences for foreign students can be to listen to fiction read aloud. This can either be complete short stories or opening chapters of longer books. The text of the story has the advantage of providing a ready-made tapescript.

Useful sources of short stories are the Macmillan Authentic Reader series: *Twentieth Century English Short Stories, British Short Stories of Today*, and the Cambridge University Press modern short stories series, e.g. *Liar* at upper intermediate level, and *A Day Saved* at advanced level. Also at advanced level are *Modern Short Stories for Students of English,* and *More Modern Short Stories for Students of English* (Oxford University Press). Sometimes Readers come with pre-recorded tapes.

In the interests of authenticity, ensure that the text is read absolutely normally as if for a native-speaker audience. Not only should the speed be normal, but there should be no attempt to pronounce words more clearly or carefully than usual, as this will lead to distortion.

Recorded radio and television programmes

In the UK and many other countries it is illegal to record network radio and television programmes for use in the classroom or for self-access. However, registered educational institutions can get permission to record certain educational programmes produced by the following organizations:

- Schools Television
- Schools Radio
- Continuing Education Television
- Continuing Education Radio

(Copying news programmes from satellite TV for educational use may be a possibility in the future.)

It is also possible to buy certain recorded programmes. Thames Television International who also have overseas agents, produce a catalogue of programmes available on video. The BBC (British Broadcasting Company) sell *Television English* which consists of short extracts from BBC television programmes accompanied by extensive printed material. In addition, the BBC produce *Newsbrief*, videos of news stories, together with transcripts and study guides. The videos appear monthly and are sent to those who take out a yearly or half-yearly subscription. It is also possible to buy *Study Tapes* from the BBC. These are recorded radio talks of a largely scientific nature.

If you do manage to build up a small library of recorded radio and television programmes, they will mostly be suitable for fairly advanced levels, since they will be authentic and unsimplified (although schools' programmes often use reasonably simple language). Store all the video and all the audio tapes together, and classify according to topic (see the section on 'Classification and access' in Chapter 1) as this will be how students will want to access this kind of material. Make sure that printed materials and recorded materials which belong together are either stored together, or are clearly linked by means of labels with the same classification mark and unique number.

Live radio and television programmes
If you can give students access to a radio or a television there are certain programmes which may be useful for them to listen to 'live'. It is a good idea to display times and wavelengths or channels of suitable programmes clearly on a notice beside the radio or television, together with a brief description of the kind of programme it is.

Perhaps the most obvious candidate for 'live' listening is the news. This is broadcast hourly on the hour by the BBC World Service, and for those in the UK, BBC Radio Four and BBC Television Channel 1. Outside Britain TV companies often broadcast programmes in English with subtitles. Students could be set a task to do at home in the evening watching their own television or listening to the radio.

It is unrealistic to try to provide support materials such as summaries and comprehension questions to accompany live programmes. Students can be advised, however, to locate the various news stories in a current newspaper and to compare this with the radio or television version. The newspaper does not

necessarily have to be an English language one, but can perfectly
well be a local newspaper. The local world news coverage can be
compared with the BBC World Service headlines and then the
students asked to identify differences of emphasis. In this way they
will be finding their own support material. Another idea is to
provide a standard review sheet which can be used for any
programme, and which students can fill in as they watch or listen
(see 3.18).

Published material
Some published material can be used for extended listening. The
characteristics which make it suitable are:

– authenticity
– correct length, i.e. not too short and not too long
– intrinsic interest
– an accompanying tapescript.

Examples of such material on audio-cassette are Scott and O'Neill
Viewpoints, Scarborough *Reasons for Listening,* Underwood *Listen to
This,* and Underwood *What a Story!* (tapescript in the teacher's
edition). On video the Cobb and Dalley *Sherlock Holmes and Dr
Watson Video Series* is just one example of published material which
is suitable for self-access listening practice.

3.14 How to use a tapescript

CLASSIFICATION   L.TA/1 = Listening. Tapescripts/1

LEVEL   **Intermediate to Advanced**

AGE   **Adolescent/adult**

ACTIVITY TYPE   **Study guide**

AIM   To show you how to use a tapescript effectively during extensive
                 listening practice.

PREPARATION   Many of the longer listening texts in the study centre or self-access
                 box have tapescripts to accompany them. A tapescript is an exact
                 written record of what is spoken on the tape. Those tapes or talks
                 which have tapescripts are marked with an asterisk ($\star$). Find a tape
                 with an accompanying tapescript now, before you look at the study
                 guide below.

STUDY GUIDE   *Introduction*: using tapescripts with longer, authentic listening texts
                 can help you in three ways:

                 1 To build up your confidence in your listening ability.
                 2 To help your comprehension.
                 3 To enable you to learn what the written words sound like.

Using tapescripts for listening practice: here are three ways of using a tapescript. The first is easiest and the last is the most difficult. Try to work your way from number 1 to number 2, and finally to number 3.

1 Read the tapescript through while you listen to the tape for the first time, thus building confidence and learning how written English sounds when spoken at normal speed. Look up any words you do not know. Now listen to the tape again without the tapescript and try to understand as much as you can.

2 Listen to the tape first without the tapescript and try to understand as much as possible. Then listen again while following the tapescript in order to fill in the bits you did not understand the first time. Perhaps you did not recognize some words you knew because of the pronunciation and the speed of speaking. If so, listen again to the pronunciation and make a note of it.

3 Listen to the tape first without the tapescript and try to understand as much as possible. Then read the tapescript silently without listening in order to fill in the bits you did not understand the first time. Finally, listen again without the tapescript and try to understand everything, referring to the tapescript again only where absolutely necessary.

Using tapescritps for pronunciation practice: if you need to practise your pronunciation, a tapescript can be useful for that too: once you have listened to the tape a few times and you understand it well, turn the volume down so that the sound is very soft and try to read with the tape. This kind of practice is known as 'shadow-reading'. It will help you with English rhythm and stress.

Comments to the teacher
You need to ensure that all your students are directed to this sheet which should form part of their learner training before they embark on any extended listening.

3.15 How to use a summary

CLASSIFICATION	**L.SU/1 = Listening. Summaries/1**
LEVEL	**Intermediate to Advanced**
AGE	**Adolescent/adult**
ACTIVITY TYPE	**Study guide**
AIM	To show you how to use a tape summary effectively during extensive listening practice.

PREPARATION

Many of the longer listening texts in the study centre or self-access box have a written summary to accompany them. A summary is not an exact written record of what is spoken on the tape, but it contains the most important points in a shortened version. Those tapes or talks which have summaries are marked with two asterisks (**). Find a tape with an accompanying summary now, before you look at the study guide below.

STUDY GUIDE

A summary can help you understand when you listen to longer texts. Here are two different ways in which you can use a summary. The second way does not give so much help as the first:

1 To prepare you for listening, read the summary before you listen. Then listen and try to understand as much as you can. Read the summary again and listen again, if necessary.

2 To check that you have understood correctly, listen to the tape first and read the summary afterwards. Listen to the tape again, if necessary.

Comments to the teacher

1 A summary can also provide a useful last step along the road to independence for advanced students in that a brief summary provides a minimum of support for listening. The less detailed a summary is, the less support it will give, and so summaries for advanced students can be graded in this way, providing progressively less and less detail.

2 Lists of difficult words and phrases which occur in the listening text are a useful supplement to summaries. Again they can be used in a variety of ways. Students can either use them to prepare themselves for the listening or they can make their own list of words and phrases as they listen, compare this at the end with the one provided.

3 As another variation, students can write their own summary and then compare what they have written with the one in the Key, or that written by another student and stored with the card. This is particularly valuable for EAP students as it gives them practice in note-taking.

3.16 How to use comprehension questions

CLASSIFICATION

L.CQ/1 = Listening. Comprehension questions/1

LEVEL

Intermediate to Advanced

AGE

Adolescent/adult

ACTIVITY TYPE

Study guide

AIM	To show you how to make effective use of comprehension questions during extensive listening practice.

PREPARATION   Many of the longer listening texts in the study centre or self-access box have comprehension questions to accompany them. Those tapes or talks which have are marked with three asterisks (★★★). Find a tape with accompanying comprehension questions now, before you look at the study guide below.

STUDY GUIDE   Comprehension questions can be used in different ways to train different listening skills. Here are three suggestions:

1 Look at the questions before you listen. In this way the questions become a focus for your listening and you can practise the skill of listening for specific information.

2 Listen to the tape and take notes while you listen. Do not look at the questions until after you have listened. Then try to answer the questions using the notes you have made. In this way you can practise listening and taking notes.

3 Listen to the tape and write some comprehension questions for the next student who uses the tape. Do not forget to leave the answers as well!

3.17 Reactive listening

CLASSIFICATION   L.RL/1 = Listening. Reactive listening/1

LEVEL   Lower intermediate to Advanced

AGE   Adolescent/adult

ACTIVITY TYPE   Listening and reacting

AIM   To listen to a dialogue, argument, discussion, etc. and to understand not only what is said, but what is really meant.

PREPARATION   There are no right or wrong answers to this activity. What is important is to consider your reaction to what you hear, and why you react in the way that you do.

INSTRUCTIONS   Listen to the tape and write down your answers to the questions below, on a separate piece of paper.

TASK SHEET   1 The speakers
- How many speakers are there?
- How many women? How many men?
- What are the names of the speakers?

- Very roughly, how old are the speakers?
- Do any of the words below apply to the speakers? If so, write
  down the word from the list, and the name of the speaker you
  think it applies to:

happy	unhappy
calm	excited
angry	friendly
ill	healthy

2 Relationships between the speakers

- Do you think any of the speakers are related (part of the same
  family)? If so, who is related to whom, and what is the
  relationship?
- Do the speakers know one another well?
- Are the speakers friends, enemies, or neither of these?
- Which speaker is the most important? Why?
- Which speaker talks the most? Why?

3 Your reactions

- Which of the speakers would you choose to spend an evening
  with? Why?
- Which of the speakers would make a reliable friend? Why?
- Which of the speakers would you turn to in an emergency? Why?
- Which of the speakers would you *not* like to meet? Why?
- Which of the speakers would you go to if you needed some advice
  on a personal matter? Why?
- Which of the speakers would you go to if you needed advice on a
  business matter? Why?

Comments to the teacher

1 This is an example of a standard listening task: it could be
applied to many different texts of recorded discussions.
Alternatively, if you feel that some of the questions might not be
appropriate for some discussions, you could have a bank of
standard questions (i.e. questions that would fit lots of different
situations) under headings such as *The speakers, The relationship
between the speakers, Your reactions,* and then for each text just select
the questions which seem most appropriate. For examples of
suitable interpretive questions for listening comprehension, see
Variations on a Theme by Alan Maley and Alan Duff.

2 As a variation, provide a number of pictures, more pictures than
there are speakers, (preferably striking pictures) and ask your
students whether they think any of them could be pictures of the
speakers. They should then justify their answer.

3.18 Programme review

CLASSIFICATION	**L.RE/1 = Listening. Review writing/1**
LEVEL	**Upper intermediate to Advanced**
AGE	**Young adult/adult**
ACTIVITY TYPE	**Listening and review writing**
AIM	To encourage reflection on programmes heard or watched, and to provide a record of programmes worth listening to or watching. To practise evaluative writing.
PREPARATION	Listen to a radio programme or watch a television programme that interests you.
INSTRUCTIONS	Use the review sheet below as a guide to writing a review of a radio or television programme you have enjoyed.

REVIEW SHEET

Programme title . . . .
Radio or television? . . . .
Wave and frequency/channel . . . .
Part of a series or 'one' off? . . . .
Title of series . . . .

Programme type (tick one)

News	☐	Current affairs	☐	Documentary	☐
Story	☐	Religion	☐	Comedy	☐
Film	☐	Practical	☐	Wild life	☐
Drama	☐	Arts review	☐	Chat show	☐
Sport	☐	Quiz show	☐	Other	☐

Topic . . . .
Description . . . .
. . . .
. . . .
Comments . . . .
. . . .
. . . .

Comments to the teacher
This is another example of a standard listening activity (see 3.17).

4 Productive skills

Introduction

The productive skills of writing and speaking present difficulties for self-access work which the receptive skills of reading and listening do not. The fundamental dilemma concerns the provision of feedback for students at the moment when they produce a stretch of language, no matter how short, which is not a predictable response. How is feedback to be provided when this happens? While it is possible to avoid this problem if one includes only activities which are self-correcting, i.e. which have only one right answer, such activities will inevitably focus on sub-skills. Useful and necessary though such practice activities may be, they are not sufficient in themselves because they do not provide practice of the whole skill. To avoid all free production activities would make for a very sterile repertoire of rather mechanical activities which would not count as 'writing' or 'speaking' in the true sense.

If free writing and speaking activities are to be included in the self-access facility, then a basic change of attitude towards teacher/student roles is required. Students have to believe that language use and practice are valuable in themselves, even when no teacher is present to evaluate their performance. They also have to develop skill and confidence in self-evaluation. For this reason, learner training guides have been included at the beginning of the 'free' writing and speaking sections in this chapter, and these are crucial to the successful introduction of what is still a fairly radical idea for most teachers and students.

In addition to the slightly problematic freer activities, however, this section contains many ideas for practising the more elementary sub-skills which go to make up the global skills of writing and speaking.

Writing

Activities which come under the heading of 'writing' can vary enormously in focus and level of difficulty. They can focus on the individual sub-skills of writing such as punctuation, or using logical connectors appropriately. Alternatively, they can focus on the global skill of communicating through writing, where a high degree of sophistication is called for, and students have to exercise many skills simultaneously. Moreover, writing activities can be highly controlled ones in which students are not required to produce original language, or they can be totally free activities in which students express themselves spontaneously with little guidance as to form. It is possible to imagine a line of difficulty upon which we can place various writing activities, for example:

Easy ←		→ Difficult
Focus on individual sub-skills. Controlled, no original production.	Focus on several sub-skills. Guided, limited production.	Focus on the global skill. Free, original production.

The first section on writing skills deals with the mechanics of writing, namely handwriting, spelling, and punctuation. The second and third sections move from controlled writing activities to more difficult guided ones, focusing on features of text organization. The final section will concentrate on 'free' writing.

Handwriting, spelling, and punctuation

Handwriting
It is obviously a good idea to include self-access activities to practise handwriting if the language of all or some of the students uses a script other than Roman. Materials can be fairly easily produced by anyone who has good, clear handwriting.

A favourite method of practice involves presenting a model to the students which they can then either copy or trace over. For beginners the model should be written on lines, as shown in 4.1 below.

Spelling
Spelling is something many students need and want to work on and it is an area where, with application, great improvements can be made by students on their own without a teacher.

In spite of the notorious unpredictability of English spelling, the aim of this section of the self-access facility should be to demonstrate areas of regularity which will help students find their way through this 'jungle'.

As an initial preparation for self-access work on spelling, a checklist can be compiled of terminology which may cause difficulty (see 4.2 and 4.3).

Punctuation
Punctuation, like spelling, is a very suitable area for self-access work. Again, like spelling, it is a good idea to have a general introduction to the section in the shape of a study guide setting out the terminology which students need to know (see 4.4, 4.5, and 4.6 below).

4.1 Fast food?

CLASSIFICATION	W.HW/1 = Writing. Handwriting/1
LEVEL	Beginner
AGE	Adolescent/adult
ACTIVITY TYPE	Copying or tracing
AIM	To practise writing English script.
EQUIPMENT	Paper with lines like this:

PREPARATION

Look at the handwriting below. Note:
1 The capital letters stand *on* the bottom solid line (_____) and reach up to the solid top line, e.g.

2 The small letters like *a*, *m*, and *r* stand *on* the bottom solid line (_____) and reach up to the dotted line (_ _ _ _), e.g.

3 The small letters with long stems like *d*, *b*, and *h* stand *on* the bottom solid line (_____). The long stem reaches up to the solid line above, and the rest of the letter reaches up to the dotted line (_ _ _ _), e.g.

4 The small letters with long tails like *g*, *p*, and *q* stand *on* the bottom solid line (____). The long tail reaches *down* to the dotted line *below* and the rest of the letter reaches up to the dotted line above, e.g.

g p q

INSTRUCTIONS   Copy the handwriting below.

TASK SHEET

An Englishman, John Montague, the
4th Earl of Sandwich, lived in the
1700s. He loved to play cards for
money, and he never liked to stop for
meals. So at the card table he often
asked for meat between two pieces
of bread.

From *Fast Food* by Lewis Jones.

Comments to the teacher

1 Remember to supply plenty of ruled paper for your students.

2 Many published materials are available for handwriting practice such as Bright and Piggott *Handwriting* and Hartley and Viney *Learn English Handwriting*.

3 If any of the students are absolute beginners then arrows can be used to show them the correct way to form and join up the letters, e.g.

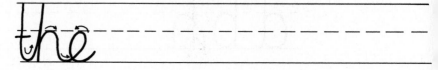

4 For more advanced writers, provide practice omitting the dotted lines.

5 Different nationalities have different handwriting and yet this is a factor which is only rarely taken into account in language teaching. Even within Europe, French handwriting is easily distinguishable from, say, German handwriting, and both are different from English handwriting. Such differences can cause real communication problems when people first encounter them, but the difficulties could be considerably lessened if students were given practice in *reading* the handwriting of the nation whose language they are studying. Such practice can easily be provided through self-access for students of English if they are given copies of texts handwritten by English people and/or Americans, etc., together with a typed copy of the same text for checking.

4.2 Important words for spelling

CLASSIFICATION	**W.SP/1 = Writing. Spelling/1**
LEVEL	**Intermediate to Advanced**
AGE	**Adolescent/adult**
ACTIVITY TYPE	**Study guide**
AIM	To teach the vocabulary necessary for learning about spelling rules.
STUDY GUIDE	To be able to follow spelling rules you need to understand words that are used in them. Here are some of the important ones:

Letter: there are twenty-six letters in the English alphabet: *a b c d e f g h i j k l m n o p q r s t u v w x y z*

Vowel: the letters *a e i o u* and sometimes *y* are the vowels of English.

Consonant: all the other letters are consonants, e.g. *b f m t*, etc.

Syllable: a part of a word, e.g. the word *today* has two syllables, i.e. *to-day*, the first syllable is *to*, the second syllable is *day*. The word *London* has two syllables, i.e. *Lon-don*, the first syllable is *Lon*, and the second syllable is *don*.

Stress: the word *toDAY* is said with more weight and more emphasis on *DAY* than on *to*. In other words, the stress is on the second syllable *DAY*. In the word *LONdon*, the stress is on the first syllable *LON*.

Prefix: a part added in front of a word to change the meaning, e.g. *un* is a prefix, *un + happy → unhappy* (= not happy), *sub* is a prefix, *sub + way → subway* (= underground passage or tunnel in British English).

Suffix: a part added at the end of a word, for instance, an adjective can be changed into an adverb, e.g. *ly* as in *slow + ly → slowly* (= in a slow manner), or a noun can be changed into an adjective, e.g. *ful* as in *hope + ful → hopeful* (= full of hope).

Comments to the teacher

1 Practice material can easily be supplied for an introductory sheet such as this, and could include such activities as picking out the vowels and consonants of words, dividing words into syllables, and underlining the stressed syllable, etc.

2 You could provide another introductory learner training guide aimed at encouraging a positive attitude to spelling, and giving reasons why correct spelling is important. Give examples of how:
- bad spelling gives a bad impression and makes the writer appear uneducated
- misspellings are sometimes confusing and/or comical
- bad spelling makes reading hard work and can, therefore, interfere with communication.

4.3 Dropping an 'l'

CLASSIFICATION	**W.SP/2 = Writing. Spelling/2**
LEVEL	**Elementary to Lower intermediate**
AGE	**Junior/adolescent**
ACTIVITY TYPE	**Study guide and practice activity**
AIM	To teach and practise the rules concerning dropping an 'l'.
STUDY GUIDE	

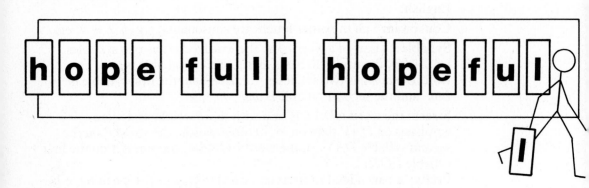

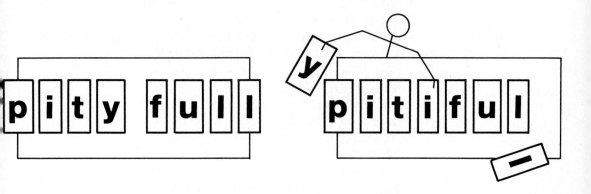

Someone who is *full of hope* is *hopeful* (with only one 'l'). Something that makes you *full of pity* is *pitiful*. *Pity* ends in 'y' after a consonant. Change 'y' into 'i' before you add the suffix *-ful*. You will see from the activity below that the suffix *-ful* does not always mean precisely *full of*, but the spelling follows the rule.

INSTRUCTIONS   Put the missing words in the sentences below. The word in brackets is your clue. Write your answers on a separate piece of paper.

TASK SHEET
1 Be . . . with that dish. (care)
2 Aeroplanes need . . . engines. (power)
3 Apples are . . . this year. (plenty)
4 It was a . . . opportunity. (wonder)
5 She measured it . . . by . . . . (spoon)
6 This is a very . . . tool. (use)
7 Remind him, he is so . . . . (forget)

KEY
1 careful   2 powerful   3 plentiful   4 wonderful
5 spoonful by spoonful   6 useful   7 forgetful

FOLLOW-UP   For more difficult spelling practice, try some dictations in the Listening section. Start with an easy one.

Comments to the teacher

1 Students will find spelling rules easier to remember if they are presented with the aid of all possible visual and graphic devices such as layout, print or letter size, colour, etc. Notice how the example above uses pin men to highlight the rule and make it visually memorable.

2 Good sources of material both for presentation and practice are spelling books for first language users such as *Learn to Spell* from which the above example is taken, or more specially for EFL, Burton *Spelling*, Burt *A Guide to Better Spelling*, Evans *Spelling Made Easy*, and Pollock *Signposts to Spelling*.

3 Other regular areas of English spelling that can be shown and practised as rules in this way include:

- the effect of silent 'e' which turns short vowels into long ones, e.g. *cap/cape, pet/Pete, fin/fine, rod/rode, cub/cube*
- formation of plurals of nouns that end in:
  's', e.g. *glass/glasses*
  'sh', e.g. *bush/bushes*
  'x', e.g. *box/boxes*
  'zz', e.g. *buzz/buzzes*
  'ch', e.g. *church/churches*
  'tch', e.g. *watch/watches*
- formation of plurals of nouns that end in 'y', i.e. if the 'y' is preceded by a vowel, add 's', e.g. *day/days*. If the 'y' is preceded by a consonant, change the 'y' into 'i' and add 'es', e.g. *baby/babies*
- dropping the silent 'e' before suffixes starting with a vowel, e.g. *hate + ing = hating.*
- doubling the last letter of one syllable words with a short vowel and ending in a single consonant when adding a suffix beginning with a vowel, e.g. *tap + ed = tapped, get + ing = getting, hid + en = hidden, hot + est = hottest, rub + er = rubber*
- 'i' before 'e' except after 'c' (but only when it rhymes with 'bee'), e.g. priest, niece, deceit, ceiling, etc.

It is also a good idea to focus specifically on some areas which seem irregular and are known to cause difficulties such as:

- silent letters, e.g. 'c' in *arctic*, or 'b' in *comb*, etc.
- unusual plurals, e.g. thief/thieves, mouse/mice, etc.
- same sound but different spelling (homophones), e.g. there/their, pair/pear, bear/bare, etc.

Lists of words in the spelling area you would like students to practice can be dictated onto a cassette. Students listen and then try to write the words they hear, with, of course, the correct spelling.

4.4 Important words for punctuation

CLASSIFICATION	**W.PU/1 = Writing. Punctuation/1**
LEVEL	**Lower intermediate to Intermediate**
AGE	**Adolescent/adult**
ACTIVITY TYPE	**Study guide**
AIM	To teach the vocabulary necessary for learning about punctuation.

STUDY GUIDE

Full stop = .	Comma = ,
Colon = :	Semi-colon = ;
Quotation marks = '. . .'	Apostrophe = '
Question mark = ?	Inverted commas = '. . .'
Hyphen = -	Exclamation mark = !
Dash = –	Brackets = (. . .)
Capital letters = A B C	

It is also a good idea to have a general introductory sheet on why punctuation is so important. The focus here is on learner training.

4.5 Why is punctuation important?

CLASSIFICATION W.PU/2 = Writing. Punctuation/2

LEVEL Lower intermediate to Intermediate

AGE Adolescent/adult

ACTIVITY TYPE Study guide and practice activity

AIM To show why good punctuation is a necessary part of communicating in writing.

STUDY GUIDE What is punctuation? It is a collection of written marks and signs to break up a string of words and make the meaning clear. They are like signposts to make it easier for someone reading to understand what you have written.

See what happens when we do not use any punctuation: good morning can i could you speak up a bit please the lines very bad okay hows that a bit better but not much i think ill call you back

Now look at the same dialogue with punctuation:
'Good morning. Can I . . . ?'
'Could you speak up a bit, please? The line's very bad.'
'Okay. How's that?'
'A bit better, but not much. I think I'll call you back.'

INSTRUCTIONS Fill in the missing punctuation in the sentences below. Write your answers on a separate sheet of paper.

TASK SHEET 1 everybody has twenty nails on each hand five and twenty on hands and feet

2 peter is a leader in the boys brigade

3 have you met my husband mrs sheridan

4 the teacher who always arrives late is mr prentice and the one whos always early is miss jacobs

5 the woman hesitated and then got off the bus drew away quickly

6 english people drink a lot of tea in the pub many of them also drink beer

7 make sure you peel that orange properly in the kitchen drawer youll find a knife to help you

8 sam wore an old red pullover jacket and shabby torn trousers

KEY

1 Everybody has twenty nails. On each hand five, and twenty on hands and feet.

2 Peter is a leader in the Boys' Brigade.

3 Have you met my husband, Mrs Sheridan?

4 The teacher who always arrives late is Mr Prentice, and the one who's always early is Miss Jacobs.

5 The woman hesitated and then got off. The bus drew away quickly.

6 English people drink a lot of tea. In the pub many of them also drink beer.

7 Make sure you peel that orange properly. In the kitchen drawer you'll find a knife to help you.

8 Sam wore an old red pullover, jacket, and shabby torn trousers.

Presentation material for punctuation should obviously be as clear, simple, and practical as possible. One way to tackle the problem is to present one feature at a time, e.g. capital letters.

4.6 Capital letters

CLASSIFICATION   W.PU/3 = Writing. Punctuation/3

LEVEL   Lower intermediate

AGE   Adolescent/adult

ACTIVITY TYPE   Study guide and practice activity

AIM   To teach and to practise the use of capital letters.

STUDY GUIDE   **1** You end a sentence with a full stop, question mark or exclamation mark. So you must start a new sentence with a capital letter, e.g. *We wandered over the plain. Occasionally a bird flew up nearby.*

2 All names of particular people, places, and things must start with a capital letter, e.g.

Admiral Smith   *London Planetarium*
Queen Elizabeth   *John Brown*
Northern Ireland   *Atlantic Ocean*

So must words coming from them, like *Elizabethan* and *Irish*. Remember, capital letters are used for particular people or things, not for the general category, e.g. *I visited three farms, one of which was Windmill Farm.*

3 Initials of people's names, or of organizations, must be in capitals, e.g.
A A Milne
BBC (British Broadcasting Corporation)
UK (United Kingdom)

4 Use capital letters for the *main* words in the titles of books, films, etc., e.g. *Farewell to Arms.*

5 Always write the word 'I' meaning *me, myself* with a capital letter.

INSTRUCTIONS

Put in capital letters where necessary in the sentences below. Write your answers on a separate sheet of paper.

TASK SHEET

1 jane didn't know the way to eastham.
2 who's that woman over there? i haven't met her.
3 we're going to two museums: the natural history museum and the british museum.
4 when we got to dover, we caught a ferry to france.
5 lord olivier is a famous actor.

KEY

1 Jane didn't know the way to Eastham.
2 Who's that woman over there? I haven't met her.
3 We're going to two museums: the Natural History Museum and the British Museum.
4 When we got to Dover, we caught a ferry to France.
5 Lord Olivier is a famous actor.

Comments to the teacher

1 As with spelling, first language materials are useful sources of ideas, but there are also specifically EFL books such as Gordon *Punctuation* and Burt *A Guide to Better Punctuation.*

2 Providing plentiful practice in punctuation does not require a lot of imagination. Simply type out a text omitting all the punctuation or use sentences illustrating the area being concentrated on.

Controlled writing activities

Controlled writing activities do not require students to actually produce any original language. They mostly involve copying, reordering or recognition activities. This means it is easy to provide feedback for students, and students (and teachers!) feel secure in this fact. On the other hand, students cannot actually learn to express themselves in writing if they restrict themselves to the activities in this section. They must, therefore, be actively encouraged to progress to the guided, and eventually, the free writing activities mentioned in later sections of this chapter.

The activities in this section have been ordered according to the amount of control or guidance the students receive, starting with the most controlled. As will be expected, the most controlled activities will tend to be the easiest. Not all controlled activities are easy, however (see, for example, 4.9).

Creative copying

Creative copying involves students in copying with a purpose as part of a problem-solving task. It is a good way to provide practice in the mechanics of writing in a way which is more interesting and challenging than mere copying out (see 4.7).

Cloze texts

Cloze texts have already featured in the Reading and Listening sections (3.1 and 3.9 respectively), with different emphases (predictive skills in 3.1 and accurate listening in 3.9). Here, in the controlled writing section, the emphasis is again slightly different: this time it is the logical connectors which are blanked out in order to focus on text structure (see 4.8).

Showing links

In this activity students are asked to circle or box grammatical referring words, for example, pronouns; reflexive pronouns; deictic adverbs such as *here, there, now, then*; substitution with *one*, etc. The point of this recognition activity is to focus attention on how such cohesive devices help to create text (see 4.9).

4.7 Furnish the house

CLASSIFICATION	W.CC/1 = Writing. Creative copying/1
LEVEL	Beginner
AGE	Junior/adolescent
ACTIVITY TYPE	Creative copying
AIM	To practise spelling and handwriting, and to revise the vocabulary of furniture and rooms in houses.

PREPARATION   Draw a big plan of a flat with a sitting-room, dining-room, kitchen, bedroom, and bathroom. Make each of the rooms big enough to write a list of words in.

INSTRUCTIONS   Below is a list of furniture and household objects. On your plan write down each item of furniture in the room where you would find it so that you finish with a list in each room. Some items may appear in more than one room. Make your lists alphabetical.

TASK SHEET

fridge	bed	settee	table
wardrobe	bath	oven	coffee table
sink	chair	armchair	bedside table
sideboard	bookcase	television	dressing table
lamp	toaster	stereo unit	washing machine
cupboard	desk	mirror	telephone

KEY

Dining-room

chair	table
lamp	telephone
sideboard	

Sitting-room

armchair	settee
bookcase	stereo unit
coffee table	television
lamp	telephone

Kitchen

cupboard
fridge
oven
sink
toaster
washing machine
telephone

Bathroom

bath
mirror
sink

Bedroom

bed
bedside table
chair
desk
dressing table
lamp
mirror
wardrobe
telephone

Comments to the teacher

1 This idea is taken from *Teaching Writing Skills* by Donn Byrne.

2 As a variation, type out a text with the sentences or paragraphs in the wrong order. Ask your students to copy out the text with all the sentences or paragraphs in the correct order. This activity is very similar to 3.2 'Sleep', under Scrambled texts in the Reading section except that, if the focus is more on writing than on reading, students can be asked to actually copy the text out rather than just say which number sentence comes first, second, third, etc.

This activity can be made quite demanding in terms of language understanding required, and this can be useful for, say, fairly fluent Arabic speakers whose handwriting is poor and needs practice.

3 Give students the opportunity to copy out texts they might wish to copy out in real life. Young students can copy out the words of pop songs, while adults can be given recipes, gardening tips, etc. to copy.

4.8 Janet's ambition

CLASSIFICATION	**W.CT/1 = Writing. Cloze text/1**
LEVEL	**Intermediate**
AGE	**Adolescent/young adult**
ACTIVITY TYPE	**Cloze text**
AIM	To focus on and practise the appropriate use of logical connectors in writing.
PREPARATION	Think about the meaning of the words in the list below and about how they are used. If you are unsure about any of them, look them up in a dictionary.
INSTRUCTIONS	Use suitable words or phrases from the list below to complete the text. You may find that there is more than one possible answer in some cases. Write your answers on a separate piece of paper.

TASK SHEET

also	since	instead	too
and	however	although	for
because	not only	in this way	for the moment
but	but also	in the meantime	in particular

Janet West's sister is an air hostess for a famous international airline. Janet wants to become one (1) . . . , (2) . . . she is still too young: the minimum age for an air hostess is twenty, (3) . . . Janet is only just over sixteen.
(4) . . . she has taken a job in an office. She (5) . . . attends evening classes. She wants to improve her French and Spanish, (6) . . . foreign languages are an essential qualification for an air hostess.
(7) . . . , Janet is gaining experience through her present job.
(8) . . . the office where she works is a travel agency, (9) . . . is she learning how to deal with people, (10) . . . quite a lot about the places she one day hopes to visit.

From *Teaching Writing Skills* by Donn Byrne.

KEY		
	1 too	**6** because/since
	2 but/although	**7** In the meantime
	3 and	**8** because/since
	4 For the moment	**9** not only
	5 also	**10** but also

FOLLOW-UP

Try one of the 'Sentence combining' activities, classification W.SC/. . . .

Comments to the teacher
For a more advanced activity, leave the students to fill in the blanks without a list.

4.9 A chance meeting

CLASSIFICATION W.SL/1 = Writing. Showing links/1

LEVEL **Intermediate to Upper intermediate**

AGE **Adult**

ACTIVITY TYPE **Marking links in a text**

AIM To focus on text organization and to practise recognition of words which refer back (or forward) to other parts of the text.

PREPARATION Read carefully through the text below and look up any words you do not understand.

INSTRUCTIONS In the text below draw a circle around the words which refer to Mrs Strickland and a box around the words referring to the narrator. They will tend to be nouns and pronouns. Some words will refer to both. The idea is to find networks in the text. The first few examples are done for you.

TASK SHEET

The season was drawing to its dusty end, and everyone $\boxed{\text{I}}$ knew was arranging to go away. (Mrs) (Strickland) was taking (her) family to the coast of Norfolk, so that the children might have the sea and (her) husband golf. (We) said goodbye to one another, and arranged to meet in the autumn. But on $\boxed{\text{my}}$ last day in town, coming out of the stores, I met her with her son and daughter; like myself, she had been making her final purchases before leaving London, and we were both hot and tired. I proposed that we should all go and eat ices in the park.

I think Mrs Strickland was glad to show me her children and she accepted my invitation with alacrity. They were even more attractive than their photographs had suggested, and she was right to be proud of them. I was young enough for them not to feel shy, and they chattered merrily about one thing and another.

From *The Moon and Sixpence* by W Somerset Maugham (1970)

KEY

The season was drawing to its dusty end, and everyone I knew was arranging to go away. Mrs Strickland was taking her family to the coast of Norfolk, so that the children might have the sea and her husband golf. We said goodbye to one another, and arranged to meet in the autumn. But on my last day in town, coming out of the stores, I met her with her son and daughter; like myself, she had been making her final purchases before leaving London, and we were both hot and tired. I proposed that we should all go and eat ices in the park.

I think Mrs Strickland was glad to show me her children and she accepted my invitation with alacrity. They were even more attractive than their photographs had suggested, and she was right to be proud of them. I was young enough for them not to feel shy, and they chattered merrily about one thing and another.

FOLLOW-UP 1	Try one of the 'Sentence combining' activities, classification W.SC/. . . .
FOLLOW-UP 2	Read the rest of this story. From time to time examine a paragraph and look for the links which bind the text together, as you did in this activity.

Comments to the teacher
This activity is designed to focus students' attention on textual cohesion. More advanced students can be asked also to draw a box around logical connectors, thus focusing on textual coherence. The circles and/or boxes can be marked beforehand so the students only have to draw arrows and show connections rather than find them.

Guided writing activities

The guided writing activities in this section are designed to provide a bridge between the controlled activities above in which students do not actually have to produce new language, and the free writing activities below where students are more or less on their own. In this section students are given the guidance they need to produce short stretches of language, and because the activities are guided rather than free, providing feedback is still relatively easy.

Sentence combining

In this activity, students are required to link individual sentences to form a coherent text. The easiest way to prepare an activity of this kind is to find a suitable text in terms of level, content, construction, etc. and then to reduce it to a number of short, unconnected sentences. Simply rewrite the text as a string of sentences leaving out backward referring words and logical connectors that could reasonably be supplied by the students. Long sentences should be divided up into shorter ones (see 4.10).

Parallel writing

This activity helps students with their writing by providing them with a model which they then attempt to emulate (see 4.11).

4.10 Wartime agriculture

CLASSIFICATION	**W.SC/1 = Writing. Sentence combining/1**
LEVEL	**Upper intermediate to Advanced**
AGE	**Adult**
ACTIVITY TYPE	**Sentence combining**
AIM	To practise text organization by combining individual sentences in such a way that they form a logical connected text.
PREPARATION	Find a short text and read it carefully. Find as many different ways as you can by which connecting words link the sentences together to form a piece of continuous writing. Words which act as connectors in this way are:

- All words which would not give you any information if they stood by themselves without the text, e.g. pronouns such as *he, they*; relative pronouns such as *who, which, that*; demonstrative pronouns such as *this, that*; words which point to a time or place such as *now, then, here, there*, etc.
- Words which show the logical relationship between one part of the text and another such as *and, but, however, in spite of that*, etc.

INSTRUCTIONS	Using appropriate connecting words, link the sentences below together to make a connected text. Although there is a model text in the key, there is not just one right answer and you should combine the sentences in the best way you can. You may choose to combine two or more sentences together. The first two sentences have been linked in one possible way as an example.

TASK SHEET

1 Farming is the oldest industry of all.

2 Farming enjoyed a brief period of prosperity during the First World War.

3 There were submarine boat attacks on merchant shipping.

4 Britain imported about two-thirds of its food.

5 It was essential to increase home food production.

6 The Government encouraged the ploughing-up of grasslands.

7 The reason for the ploughing-up of grasslands was to grow more cereals.

8 The Government gained the co-operation of farmers in 1917.

9 The farmers co-operated because the Government gave them guaranteed prices in 1917.

10 In 1917 agricultural workers were given a reasonable minimum wage.

11 The wheat harvest was increased by sixty per cent.

12 There was a large rise in the production of potatoes, barley, and oats.

EXAMPLE

Farming, the oldest industry of all, enjoyed a brief period of prosperity during the First World War. (Sentences 1 & 2)

KEY

Original text
Farming, the oldest industry of all, enjoyed a brief period of prosperity during the First World War. Submarine boat attacks on merchant shipping, at a time when Britain imported about two-thirds of its food, made it essential to increase home food production. The Government encouraged the ploughing-up of grassland in order to grow more cereals, and gained the co-operation of farmers by giving them guaranteed prices in 1917. In the same year, agricultural workers were given a reasonable minimum wage. The wheat harvest was increased by sixty per cent, and there was a large rise in the production of potatoes, barley, and oats.

Adapted from *Britain since 1700* by R J Cootes & L E Snellgrove.

4.11 Europe

CLASSIFICATION   W.PW/1 = Writing. Parallel writing/1

LEVEL   Lower intermediate

AGE   Young adult/adult

ACTIVITY TYPE   Parallel writing

AIM   To practise writing short connected texts with the help of a model text.

PREPARATION

Read this short description of Hungary:

Hungary is between Austria and Rumania. Czechoslovakia is to the north and Yugoslavia is to the south. There are 10,200,000 people in Hungary. The capital, Budapest, is on the River Danube and has a population of 1,900,000.

Notice how the text is organized. (The information is taken from the map below.) In what order do the following facts appear?
– the population of the capital
– the population of the country
– the name of the capital
– the geographical position of the country
– the name of the river on which the capital stands.

INSTRUCTIONS

Using the text on Hungary as a model to help you, write a similar description of the following places:

1 Austria
2 Bulgaria
3 Poland
4 Switzerland

Get the information you need from the map below.

TASK SHEET

EUROPE		
Country	**Capital**	**River**
Austria	Vienna	Danube
(7,400,000)	(1,600,000)	
Bulgaria	Sofia	Iskŭr
(8,000,000)	(700,000)	
Poland	Warsaw	Vistula
(32,500,000)	(1,200,000)	
Switzerland	Berne	Aare
(6,000,000)	(170,000)	

KEY

1 Austria
Austria is between Switzerland and Hungary. West Germany and Czechoslovakia are to the north and Italy and Yugoslavia are to the south. There are 7,400,000 people in Austria. The capital, Vienna, is on the River Danube and has a population of 1,600,000.

2 Bulgaria
Bulgaria is between Yugoslavia and the Black Sea. Rumania is to the north and Greece is to the south. There are 8,000,000 people in Bulgaria. The capital, Sofia, is on the River Iskŭr and has a population of 700,000 people.

3 Poland
Poland is between East Germany and the USSR. The Baltic Sea is to the north and Czechoslovakia is to the south. There are 32,500,000 people in Poland. The capital, Warsaw, is on the River Vistula and has a population of 1,200,000.

4 Switzerland
Switzerland is between France and Austria. West Germany is to the north and Italy is to the south. There are 6,000,000 people in Switzerland. The capital, Berne, is on the River Aare and has a population of 170,000.

Comments to the teacher
The technique of parallel writing is described in detail in *Teaching Written English* by Ron White. Basically the technique can be summarized as follows:

- Give students a model text based on data to which they also have access. The original data can be in the form of notes, a diagram, a map, a picture, etc.
- Set students questions to answer or a task to perform which focuses on the key features of the type of text in question, e.g. in a narrative text, the language used to sequence events in time and/or present the chain of cause and effect.
- Give students similar data on a different topic and ask them to produce a similar text to the model.

Free writing activities

Is it practicable to have a free writing section for self-access? The answer to this question partly depends on the kind of students involved – how independent and well-motivated they are – and on the kind of preparation and training students are given.

Study guides
An initial study guide on writing can give students some idea of what they can do on their own (see 4.12 and 4.13).

Summary writing

Providing a written or spoken summary of a long text is a very demanding task. In spite of this, students are frequently required to write summaries with little or no guidance as to how to go about the task. EAP and ESP students, in particular, frequently need to summarize information in the course of their jobs or studies. Below is an example of how students can be taken step-by-step through the processes of information extraction and summary (see 4.14).

Story writing

If students are going to attempt to write imaginatively inside or outside the classroom it is extremely important that the instructions given are detailed and clear, and that the topics themselves contain plenty of ideas to stimulate the imagination.

Pictures are a good way of providing the all-important context for story-writing, and magazine pictures or advertisements are an excellent source of ideas for writing workcards. Below are two examples based on advertisement pictures: in the first students are prompted to create their own context by a series of questions to which they must decide the answers; in the second, the technique is used of beginning a story and asking students to continue it (see 4.15 and 4.16).

4.12 Improving your written English

CLASSIFICATION W.FW/1 = Writing. Free writing/1

LEVEL Intermediate to Advanced

AGE Adolescent/adult

ACTIVITY TYPE Study guide

STUDY GUIDE This study guide gives you some ideas for improving your writing by working on your own without a teacher.

1 Do not expect to write everything correctly the first time. Always produce at least one draft and have the patience to review it, and rewrite it as often as necessary. Even native speakers do this.

2 Do not rely on teachers to improve *your* writing. They can give you valuable help but the only person who can actually make a difference to your writing is *you*. Accept your responsibility in learning to write better English and do not just wait for the teacher to mark your work.

3 Any word whose spelling you are not absolutely sure about should be checked in a dictionary. Do not guess if you have any doubt at all.

4 Look back over a number of pieces of your written work which have been marked by a teacher. How many careless mistakes were there on average in each piece?

5 Find a friend whose English is about the same level as yours and arrange to check each other's written work. Can you find each other's careless mistakes?

6 Be a critical reader. Notice when you read how writers achieve their desired effect in English. Collect phrases or words that particularly impress you and write them down in a notebook.

Comments to the teacher

Even in a classroom situation where students will have their written work corrected, a study guide like the one above can do a lot to increase the student's responsibility for their own writing. For more ideas on how to focus on the process of writing see *Writing* by Tricia Hedge, in this series.

4.13 Writing for real

CLASSIFICATION   **W.FW/2 = Writing. Free writing/2**

LEVEL   **Intermediate to Advanced**

AGE   **Adolescent/adult**

ACTIVITY TYPE   **Study guide**

STUDY GUIDE   Who do you write English to or for apart from your teacher?

Does your writing suffer from severely limited readership? Does your written work come back from your teacher with an outbreak of mysterious little red marks all over it? Break free! Write to someone else for a change. Here are some suggestions:

1 Write to yourself – keep a diary in English. Write down all your secret thoughts and fears about learning English!

2 Find an English-speaking pen-friend and write letters to him or her.

3 Write an article, a poem, or a short story for the school English magazine.

4 Write or reply to an open letter for our correspondence board.

5 Write to a newspaper, published in English, in your country.

6 Write a commentary for other students on a book you have read from the library. We can add it to the 'book reviews' file.

7 Find other students who want to practise in English and form a writers' club. Write for one another.

Comments to the teacher

1 The above suggestions for the students presuppose a certain amount of help and organization on the part of teachers in the following areas:

- *pen-friends*: organize an English pen-friend agency in your school or college
- *the English magazine*: organize a regular English magazine in your school or college. Make sure that most, if not all, editorial responsibility lies with the students
- *correspondence board*: provide a board somewhere purely for students to display open letters to one another and/or to teachers
- *book reviews*: provide a clearly labelled file for students' own reviews of books they have read (see 3.6)
- *writers' club*: encourage the formation of such clubs and give help and advice to enable students to find someone of their own English level and interests to write to.

2 In addition to the above suggestions the institution can arrange for regular writing competitions to be judged by a committee of students, rather than by staff. All the institution needs to provide is encouragement and guidance as to how to organize and publicize the event, and a little money for a prize.

4.14 The Yega

CLASSIFICATION	W.SU/1 = Writing. Summarizing/1
LEVEL	Advanced
AGE	Young adult/adult
ACTIVITY TYPE	Summary writing
AIM	To practise writing a summary of a long text.
PREPARATION	Read through the passage and look up any words you do not understand.
INSTRUCTIONS	1 Read the passage below and, starting with the third paragraph:

- put a box round the names of villages and settlements
- circle the base + ed verbs for each move of the Yega through their territory
- number these verbs in sequence, beginning with number 1
- underline the words which tell when each move took place.

2 Now read the passage again, but this time:
- number the places on the map in the order (or sequence) in which the Yega moved there
- draw a line on the map indicating the path of Yega movements during the period discussed.

3 Read the passage a third time and:
- read for information needed to fill in the table (Population Movements among the Yega)
- complete the table.

4 Write a summary of the text based on the information on the map and the table. Do not look back to the passage.

5 Check your own summary against the model summary given in the key.

TASK SHEET

Settlement patterns of the Yega

Time	Moved from	To	Reasons for moving
Pre European		Basabuga	
1930			
	All villages		
			The end of the war
		Inland villages	

Population movements among the Yega

The Yega

The Yega is a group of nearly 900 people living in sixteen settlements, on an area of about twelve square miles, on the north coast of Papua. They live on a gently sloping alluvial plain between Mount Lamington and the sea. During the last seventy years there have been a number of changes in the economic and social life of the Yega, and the economic changes in particular have brought about considerable changes in the pattern of settlement. Although most development has occurred in the last twenty years, there is evidence, supported by the oral traditions of Yega elders, to show that some evolution of settlement had occurred even before the first contact with white men.

By tradition, the Yega were sea people. This probably means that long ago they arrived as migrants and originally spent most of their time aboard their canoes and that they lived mainly upon seafood. They settled first on three small islands, Baroda Deuga, about half a mile north-east of Wasusu. These islands are composed entirely of coarse coral sand and lumps of dead coral. Although there are mangrove trees on the islands, there is no possibility of growing food crops there, and this would have been true in earlier times.

At some time well before the arrival of white men, the Yega moved from Baroda Deuga and founded a village, Basabuga, on the eastern shore of Wasusu Point. In Basabuga each clan was allocated a specified area in which family heads built their homes. Probably there were only three original clans, but these were joined at intervals by ancestors of the other five clans who make up the Yega parish. Basabuga is on an ideal defensive site, protected on the landward side by mangrove swamps to the south-east, and on the south-western side by swamp-filled depressions running parallel to the beach. The sea provided an escape route to the north.

Up to 1910 when the first school was begun at Wasusu Point, some clans moved eastward or westward and settled in other coastal villages, such as Tarebosusu and Kanunje. The main reason for the dispersal of clans from Basabuga was probably population pressure; but the enforced cessation of interparish warfare undoubtedly contributed. The movement westward along the beach from Tarebosusu to Beporo and Gona continued until about 1930. People were encouraged to move by the increasing effectiveness of government control and by the establishment at Gona Mission of a school and hospital staffed by Europeans. The new coastal village sites also reduced walking time to the gardens.

The war of 1939–45 affected the Yega in several important ways. Their territory became one of the major battlefields of the Pacific War. Every person migrated from the area. Most of the able-bodied men went away to serve in the army or labour corps, while the women and children shifted to another Anglican mission about thirty miles to the north.

When they returned at the end of the war, they found everything destroyed. They were paid some compensation. Meanwhile, the war had brought with it new experiences and changes in attitudes among the younger men. In addition, the transfer of administrative headquarters from Buna to Higatutu resulted in the construction of a major road to the port of Cape Killerton, and this brought the Yega into closer touch with the outside world than ever before. As a result, between 1945 and 1950, about twenty families left their rebuilt villages between Gona and Basabuga and they moved east to found the new village of Surilai at Cape Killerton. Men living at Surilai have since found regular employment on the government wharf at Cape Killerton.

Since 1960, seven new inland villages have been established along the road leading from Gona Mission to the town of Popondetta. This movement inland from the coast was initiated by the development of a cocoa-planting project. As the cocoa blocks were a long walk from their homes in Beporo village, many people moved inland, and by 1964, over half the Yega population was living in the new villages to the south of Gona and Beporo. (Adapted from R. B. Dakeyne, *Village and Town in New Guinea*. Longman.)

From *Teaching Written English* by Ron White.

KEY

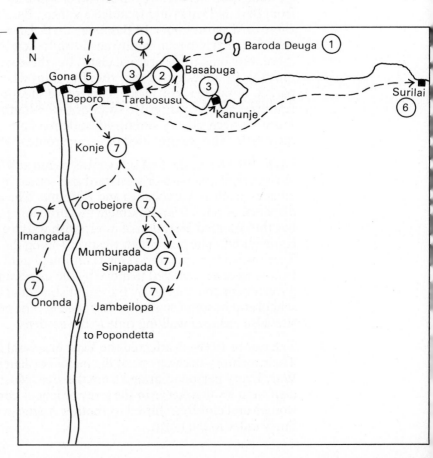

Time	Moved from	To	Reasons for moving
Pre European	Baroda Deuga	Basabuga	Couldn't grow crops
Pre 1910	Basabuga	Tarebosusu Kanunje	Population pressure No more wars
1930	Tarebosusu	Beporo, Gona	Effective govt. control Gona mission school
1939–45	All villages	Men → army labour camps Women → north	Area became a battlefield
1945	Villages between Gona and Basabuga	Gona, Beporo	The end of the war
1945–50		Surilai	New road to Cape Killerton, port employment
Since 1960	Coastal villages	Inland villages	Cocoa planting project

Model summary

Long before the arrival of Europeans, the Yega were settled on three islands, Baroda Deuga, situated just off the northern coast. No crops could be grown on these islands, so the tribe moved to Basabuga on the mainland coast, a spot ideally situated for defence. Once the cessation of intertribal wars removed the need for strong defence, increasing population growth caused the Yega to move west along the coast to the villages of Tarebosusu and Kanunje. This was prior to 1910, still before the arrival of any Europeans. From 1910 to 1930 more efficient government controls, together with the opening of a mission school in Gona, caused the Yega to migrate from Tarebosusu further west along the coast to settle in the villages of Beporo and Gona.

The 1939–45 war caused all the Yega to leave the area. The men went into the army while the women and children went to stay in an Anglican mission 30 miles to the north. At the end of the war they returned to rebuild the ruined villages of Gona and Basabuga. Between 1945 and 1950, they founded the new village of Surilai along the coast to the east on the new road to Cape Killerton. Men living at Surilai can find regular employment at the port of Cape Killerton. Since 1960 many of the Yega have moved inland from the coast to new villages near the cocoa plantation which provides them with employment. There are now seven inland villages along the road from Gona to Popondetta.

Comments to the teacher

Students who are studying English for Academic Purposes can bring in their own texts and either they or you can devise charts, maps, diagrams, etc. for an information-transfer activity like the one above. The students can then write their summaries based on the information extracted, and, if they wish, leave a copy of their summary in the activity folder for other students to compare with their own.

4.15 A nasty surprise

CLASSIFICATION   **W.SW/1 = Writing. Story writing/1**

LEVEL   **Intermediate to Advanced**

AGE   **Young adult/adult**

ACTIVITY TYPE   **Story writing**

AIM   To practise imaginative free writing in English.

PREPARATION   Have you ever had anything stolen? Worse still, have you ever had your money and passport stolen while you were on holiday abroad? This is just what happened to the unfortunate couple in the picture below.

INSTRUCTIONS   Write a letter telling the story behind the picture. There are some questions to guide you.

TASK SHEET

1 Who is the letter to? A newspaper? An insurance company? A friend? A relative?

2 Who are you? One of the people in the picture? A friend or relative of someone in the picture?

3 Where are the people in the picture? How did they get there? Why are they there?

4 What will happen next? How will the people in the picture feel? What will they say and do?

5 What problems will there be and how will they be overcome?

6 Will the ending to this story be happy or unhappy?

7 Will the people in the story behave any differently in future?

4.16 A strange move

LASSIFICATION   W.SW/2 = Writing. Story writing/2

EVEL   Intermediate to Advanced

GE   Adolescent

CTIVITY TYPE   Story writing

IM   To practise imaginative free writing in English.

REPARATION   Have you ever felt really bored and wished something extraordinary could happen to you? What would you do if it really did?

ISTRUCTIONS   Look at the picture and read the beginning of the story below. Your task is to write an ending to the story.

ASK SHEET

Mr and Mrs Wilson and their two children, Frank and Janet, were an ordinary English family living in an ordinary English family house in an ordinary English street. Mr Wilson caught the train to the office every day. Mrs Wilson worked in a shop and Frank and Janet went to school. Their lives were rather boring, that is, until one day . . .

It was a damp and miserable Monday morning in the middle of January and the Wilson family were having their breakfast in gloomy silence. As coincidence would have it, they were all thinking the same thing at the same time: the summer holidays seemed so far away!

Suddenly, they heard a strange roaring noise and as they looked at one another in surprise, they felt themselves rising as if they were in a lift! The upward movement stopped and the family looked around. They could see nothing out of the windows but white walls. Then they felt a movement again like the thrust of an aeroplane. Mr and Mrs Wilson stared at one another in terror . . .

Comments to the teacher

1 Provide the students with a number of imaginative writing topics which they can use for self-access writing, if they wish. (Even in a traditional classroom situation allowing individual students to choose their own topics will give them more freedom in their writing than is usually the case.)

2 It is a good idea to provide an imaginative writing display board somewhere where students can display and share their work with others. If we are trying to wean them away from the idea that they can only write for a teacher, we have to provide them with possibilities for an alternative readership.

3 As a variation, create writing workcards for other genres of writing which cater for the needs and interests of your particular students. Here are some suggestions:
- business letters
- informal and formal reports
- autobiographical or biographical accounts
- advertisements
- an election manifesto
- descriptions of people, places, processes
- criticism of local concerts, plays, etc.

(Make sure you classify these workcards by text-type and create a text-type index for writing so that it is easy for students to find work on a particular kind of writing.)

4 As well as using pictures as a stimulus to writing, the following stimuli could also be used:
- visual information such as graphs, charts, diagrams
- accounts, balance sheets, etc.
- newspaper and magazine articles
- letters which have to be replied to.

Speaking

Speaking, like writing, involves an enormous range of sub-skills. Some of these sub-skills involve the mechanics of sound production, i.e. pronunciation, and these sub-skills will be the focus for the first section on speaking. Other speaking skills involve fluent and accurate expression of meaning, the exercising of pragmatic, or communicative, competence, and the observance of the rules of appropriacy. All of these skills together may be said to make up the global skill of speaking as an act of communication and interaction with others, and these will be the focus of the second section.

Pronunciation

Pronunciation is a difficult skill for students to improve entirely on their own. Most foreign students cannot listen critically to their own performance or diagnose their problems with any precision.

It is possible to give students some guidance by organizing and classifying activities according to language group, and to state in each activity which language groups tend to have the particular pronunciation difficulty focused on. The ideal situation, however, is that students have access to a teacher who can assess and advise on their particular pronunciation needs and guide students into using the self-access system to their best advantage. It should also be emphasized that frequent exposure to native-speaker speech is necessary for the students to make real and lasting progress in speaking, so that many of the activities in the listening section are relevant to improving speaking skills (see 3.14 in the listening section).

Individual sounds

The aim of this section of the self-access facility will be to provide students with help in their efforts to correct individual sound production problems which may hinder communication.

Material designed to help students produce difficult sounds should ideally contain an information guide which introduces them to the terminology and diagrammatic representations they are going to meet in working on pronunciation (see 4.17 and 4.18).

Word Stress

Word stress is arguably the most critical area of pronunciation in that native speakers rely very heavily on the auditory 'shape' of words, i.e. the number and combination of stressed and unstressed syllables, for recognition and comprehension. Errors in word stress are more likely to lead to a breakdown in communication than any other kind of pronunciation error.

To begin with students should consult a study guide to ensure that they understand the terminology which they will come across when studying word stress such as *vowel, consonant, syllable, stress, prefix,* and *suffix*. In fact, all these words are explained in 4.2 (the study guide for Spelling), and there is no reason why that guide cannot be slightly adapted for the word stress section.

Many students feel that word stress in English is very difficult. They build up a mental block concerning it and the best way to combat this defeatist attitude and restore student confidence is to produce materials which clearly highlight areas of regularity in English word stress such as the effect of the various affixes on word stress (see 4.19 and 4.20).

Compound word stress

One of the most difficult areas of word stress is the question of where to place stress in compound words, especially compound nouns. These words are very common in English. Unfortunately, some of the rules are very complicated. The best thing is to allow students to discover patterns for themselves through carefully devised discovery tasks (see 4.21).

Rhythm and stress

English rhythm and stress are two of the hardest aspects of English pronunciation for many students to master. Germanic languages such as English combine stressed and unstressed syllables to achieve their characteristic rhythm pattern. In order to give students practice in hearing the difference between stressed and unstressed syllables, and also to make them aware of the kinds of words which are stressed, present them with a dialogue or text with the rhythm marked (including pauses) and let them hear the text read on cassette (see 4.22).

4.17 Words for pronunciation

CLASSIFICATION	S.IS/1 = Speaking. Individual sounds/1
LEVEL	Beginner to Lower intermediate
AGE	Adolescent/adult
ACTIVITY TYPE	Study guide
AIM	To teach the words needed for studying pronunciation.
INSTRUCTIONS	Learn the words below, which you will need to know in order to study how to make English sounds:
STUDY GUIDE	

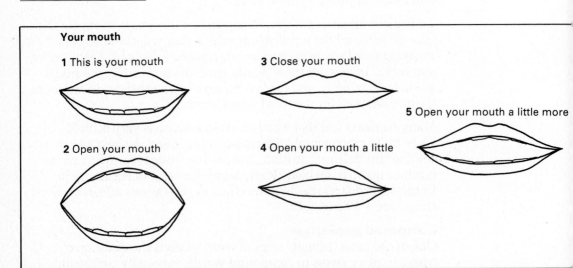

Your mouth

1 This is your mouth

2 Open your mouth

3 Close your mouth

4 Open your mouth a little

5 Open your mouth a little more

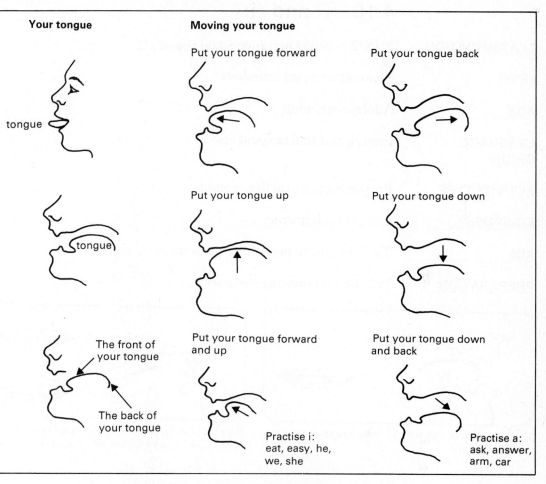

Your tongue

tongue

tongue

The front of your tongue

The back of your tongue

Moving your tongue

Put your tongue forward

Put your tongue back

Put your tongue up

Put your tongue down

Put your tongue forward and up

Practise i:
eat, easy, he,
we, she

Put your tongue down and back

Practise a:
ask, answer,
arm, car

From *Ship or Sheep?* by Anne Baker.

Comments to the teacher
Task sheets on the individual sounds should deal with only one sound, or one sound contrast, at a time. For each sound there should be:

– a written description of the position of the articulatory organs
– a diagram showing a cross-section of the oral cavity with the position of the articulatory organs
– a photograph or drawing showing the outward setting of lips, teeth, tongue, upper and lower jaw, etc.
– a recording of the sound or sounds in question
– a list of words containing the sound(s) for practice together with a recording of the list.

Below is a task sheet which contains all of the above. It has been adapted from *Ship or Sheep?* by Anne Baker which, together with *Tree or Three?* also by Anne Baker, is an excellent source of material for individual sound practice.

4.18 /i/ and /i:/

CLASSIFICATION	S.IS/2 = Speaking. Individual sounds/2
LEVEL	Elementary to intermediate
AGE	Adolescent/adult
LANGUAGE GROUP	French and Italian speakers
ACTIVITY TYPE	Pronunciation practice (sounds)
EQUIPMENT	A small hand mirror.
AIM	To show how to pronounce the sounds /i/ and /i:/.
PREPARATION	Practise pronouncing these sounds:

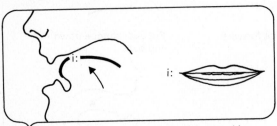

Open your mouth very little to make the sound i :.
i : is a long sound.

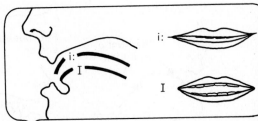

First practise the sound i :. Then open your mouth
little more. i : is a long sound. I is a short sound

INSTRUCTIONS   Listen to the tape and repeat what you hear.

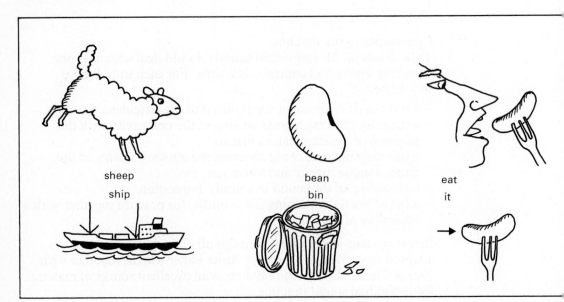

sheep
ship

bean
bin

eat
it

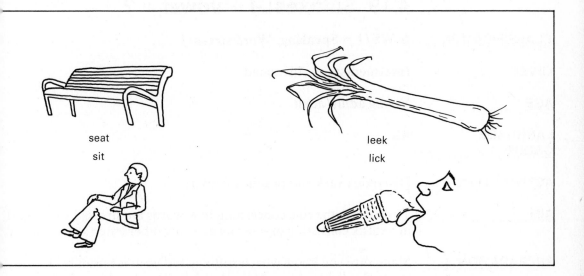

seat

sit

leek

lick

OLLOW-UP The minimal pairs activities in the Listening section will also help you improve your pronunciation (see those activities with the classification L.MP/. . .).

Comments to the teacher

1 Sounds which may by some be considered deviant in standard southern English but which occur quite readily in other accents of English, are best avoided. These include such things as: light 'l' in medial and final position, e.g. in 'old' and 'all' (as in Welsh English); the pronunciation of 'r' after a vowel, e.g. in 'turn' (prevalent in Scotland, the West Country, America, etc); the articulation of 'g' in the 'ing' combination, e.g. in 'sing' (common in parts of the North of England), etc. Concentrate your resources instead on sound contrasts which really do matter in English such as /i/ and /i:/, /p/ and /b/, /l/ and /r/, etc.

2 Note the inclusion of a hand mirror as necessary equipment for students practising individual sounds.

3 Note also the added classification of 'language group' in this section to facilitate student access. With the aid of a list or a card index, it should be possible for students to search for activities for a particular language group. An information sheet setting out the typical difficulties of the various language groups who use the facility and the reference numbers of the 'packs' which focus on those particular difficulties, will give students easy access to what they need.

4 If facilities for making and viewing videos are available, then video recordings of people pronouncing sounds and words can be made and students encouraged to use the 'freeze frame' facility to observe in detail the outward appearance and movement of the lower face.

4.19 Suffixes: -i + vowel + ?

CLASSIFICATION	S.WS/1 = Speaking. Word stress/1
LEVEL	**Intermediate to Advanced**
AGE	**Young adult/adult**
LANGUAGE GROUP	**All**
ACTIVITY TYPE	**Discovery task and practice activity**

AIM

To discover the rule concerning how words are stressed which end in a suffix consisting of -i + vowel + any other letter(s) or no letter.

PREPARATION

Make sure you know what a suffix is and what is meant by a stressed syllable. Also, do you know what a vowel is and what a consonant is? If you wish to check first, see 4.2.

INSTRUCTIONS

1 On a separate piece of paper, using a dictionary if you need to, write down the words below and mark their stress pattern. Use a big 'O' for the stressed syllable and a small 'o' for any other syllable. For example, *banana* has the stress pattern *oOo*. The first example below has already been done for you. You may find it easier to separate the word into its syllables first.

2 Now write down the suffix of each word. Again, the first one has been done for you.

TASK SHEET 1

Word	Stress	Suffix
in-flat-ion	*oOo*	*-ion*
magnification		
isolation		
regulation		
damnation		
circulation		
relation		
education		
admiration		

3 Now answer these questions:
– Can you see a word stress rule at work here?
– If so, what is the rule?

Word	Stress	Suffix
in-flat-ion	oOo	-ion
mag-ni-fi-cat-ion	oooOo	-ion
i-so-lat-ion	ooOo	-ion
re-gu-lat-ion	ooOo	-ion
dam-nat-ion	oOo	-ion
cir-cu-lat-ion	ooOo	-ion
re-lat-ion	oOo	-ion
e-du-cat-ion	ooOo	-ion
ad-mi-rat-ion	ooOo	-ion

- There is a rule here.
- Words which end in the suffix *-ion* are stressed on the syllable before the suffix.

TASK SHEET 2

1 The instructions are the same as those for task sheet 1.

Word	Stress	Suffix
recipient	*oOoo*	*-ient*
deviant		
substantial		
invention		
median		
infectious		
familiar		
radius		
mania		
deviate		
pecuniary		
negotiable		
premium		
superior		
radio		
provision		

2 Now answer these questions:
- In what way are all the suffixes the same?
- In each word, where does the stressed syllable come?
- Is the rule above (in task sheet 1) still correct?

Word	Stress	Suffix
recipient	oOoo	-ient
deviant	Ooo	-iant
substantial	oOo	-ial
invention	oOo	-ion
median	Ooo	-ian
infectious	oOo	-ious
familiar	oOO	-iar
radius	Ooo	-ius
mania	Ooo	-ia

deviate	Ooo	-iate
pecuniary	oOoo	-iary
negotiable	oOoo	-iable
premium	Ooo	-ium
superior	oOoo	-ior
radio	Ooo	-io
provision	oOo	-ion

- All the suffixes begin with an 'i' followed by a vowel, followed optionally by a consonant, vowel, or nothing. We can express this by means of the formula: 'i' + vowel + ?
- In each word the stressed syllable comes immediately *before* the suffix.
- The rule above was 'Words which end in the suffix *-ion* are stressed on the syllable before the suffix.' This rule is correct, but it does not go far enough. In fact the rule is 'Words which end in an 'i' + vowel + ? suffix are stressed on the syllable *before* the suffix.'

Comments to the teacher

1 For other rules and areas of regularity in word stress see Kenworthy *Teaching English Pronunciation*, and also 'Spelling in TESL: Stress Cues to Vowel Quality' by W B Dickerson and R H Finney in *TESOL Quarterly*, Vol 12/2.

2 In addition to focusing on the more regular areas of word stress, it is also a good idea to deal with the areas which always cause difficulty such as those words that shift stress depending on their grammatical function, e.g. *'advertise* (verb), *ad'vertisement* (noun). There is particular difficulty in cases where the written form remains the same and only the stress changes, e.g. *re'cord* (verb), *'record* (noun); *con'flict* (verb), *'conflict* (noun); *dis'pute* (verb), *'dispute* (noun), etc.

So far in this section the emphasis has been on a problem-solving approach to English word stress. It is also possible, of course, to devise large numbers of task sheets which are basically self-tests. These can consist simply of lists of polysyllabic words and students can be asked to indicate stress patterns either by marking the stress or by sorting the words into sets according to whether the stress falls on the first, second, third, etc. syllable. Such practice activities may not promote learning to the same degree as a discovery task like the one above, but they can at least serve to show students where there are gaps in their knowledge.

4.20 Word stress activity

CLASSIFICATION	S.WS/2 = Speaking. Word stress/2
LEVEL	**Intermediate**
AGE	**Adolescent/adult**
ACTIVITY TYPE	**Practice activity**
AIM	To practise recognition of stressed syllables in words.
PREPARATION	All words of two or more syllables have one syllable that is stressed more than the other(s). We will call this the stressed syllable. The word *yesterday* has three syllables and it is the first syllable which is the stressed one. We can show this by writing the stressed syllable in capital letters, e.g. *YES-ter-day*. We can also say that this word *yesterday* has the stress pattern: stressed – unstressed – unstressed. Another, quicker, way of saying this stress pattern would be *TUM – ti – ti*, where *TUM* stands for the stressed syllable and *ti* stands for any unstressed syllable.

INSTRUCTIONS

1 Looks at the following words. They are grouped into three different stress patterns:

ti – TUM – ti	TUM – ti – ti	ti – ti – TUM
en – GAGE – ment	WON – der – ful	af – ter – NOON
a – LARM – ing	RI – di – cule	un – der – STAND

2 Copy down the three lists on a piece of paper and add each word below to the correct column, depending on its stress pattern.

TASK SHEET

umbrella	ambulance	elephant	margarine
national	scandalous	tomorrow	insincere
harmony	remember	enjoyment	fantastic

KEY

ti – TUM – ti	TUM – ti – ti	ti – ti – TUM
um – BREL – la	AM – bu – lance	mar – gar – INE
to – MOR – row	E – le – phant	in – sin – CERE
re – MEM – ber	NA – tion – al	
en – JOY – ment	SCAN – da – lous	
fan – TAS – tic	HAR – mo – ny	

Comments to the teacher

1 Remember to use only words where the stress is fixed and unambiguous. If you wish to include words like *record*, then the word must be contextualized in a sentence to show whether it is the noun or the verb form which is being tested.

2 Another good way of providing self-test material on word stress is to use visuals as cues, thus testing vocabulary as well as word stress. Pictures from magazines can be pasted on to individual cards, the word for the object written on the back of the card, showing the correct stress. Or a number of pictures can be pasted on a single worksheet, with the answers on the back. Holden *Materials for Language Teaching – Interaction Packages A & B* are one source of small pictures, as are magazines, and catalogues. The words can also be recorded onto cassette if facilities are available, so that students can hear the correct stress as well as seeing the picture.

4.21 Two kinds of compound noun

CLASSIFICATION

S.CW/1 = Speaking. Compound words/1

LEVEL

Upper intermediate to Advanced

AGE

Adolescent/adult

LANGUAGE GROUP

All

ACTIVITY TYPE

Discovery task

AIM

To discover how two different kinds of compound noun differ in their stress patterns.

PREPARATION

1 In English two (or more) nouns can be used together to convey one idea – one meaning. A lot of these 'joined' nouns have become one word, as in *bedroom*, and *teapot*, but many of them remain two separate words and they are then known as compound nouns. They are very common in English. There are many established compounds such as *railway station*, or *school bus* but, in addition, native speakers frequently create new ones.

2 Compound nouns which consist of two nouns can be divided into two categories: those where the first word takes the main stress, and those where the second word takes the main stress. How can you know where to put the stress in compound nouns?

INSTRUCTIONS

Sort the following compound nouns into two different groups according to whether the main stress falls on the first or second word, and then try to answer the questions which follow. Use a dictionary, if necessary.

apple pie	paper weight	stone wall	apple tree
pork butcher	lace curtain	paper bag	pork chop
stone quarry	gold leaf	lace maker	gold rush

Now check your answers by looking at part one of the key. Compare the pairs of words that have one word in common, like *apple pie* and *apple tree*. What explanation could there be for the difference in stress patterns? Where would you expect the main stress to fall in the following compounds? Why?

| plum jam | plum stone | diamond necklace | diamond mine |
| silk shirt | silk worm | brick wall | brick factory |

Stress on the first word	**Stress on the second word**
apple tree	apple pie
paper weight	paper bag
stone quarry	stone wall
pork butcher	pork chop
lace maker	lace curtain
gold rush	gold leaf

Notice that where the stress falls on the second word, the first word in the compound describes what the second one is made of, e.g. an *apple pie* is made of apples in a way that an *apple tree* is not; a *pork chop* is made of pork whereas a *pork butcher* cuts and sells pork. The same difference can be seen in the following pairs of words:

Stress on the first word	**Stress on the second word**
plum stone	plum jam
diamond mine	diamond necklace
silk worm	silk shirt
brick factory	brick wall

4.22 A time to be born

S.RS/1 = Speaking. Rhythm and stress/1

Intermediate to Advanced

Young adult/adult

French, Italian, Spanish, Portuguese, Chinese, Japanese speakers

Recognition activity, repetition, and discovery task

1 To improve the ability to hear the difference between stressed and unstressed syllables.

2 With the help of a model to practise reading a dialogue with correct rhythm and stress.

3 To discover which kinds of words are stressed and which unstressed.

INSTRUCTIONS

1 Look at the dialogue below. The slashes (/) show that the following syllable is stressed. Pauses are marked: ʌ. As you listen to the dialogue, try and hear the stresses and the pauses. Then listen again and repeat after the tape. Finally, listen once more and try to read with the tape.

2 Look again at the dialogue. What sort of words are stressed, and what sort of words are not stressed?

TASK SHEET

A /ʌ Is there / sugar in it?
B /ʌ You pre/fer it with / sugar in it.
A /ʌ Yes, I / usually / do, but it's / recently been / making me a / bit / sick.
B /ʌ Are you / comfortable?
A /Reasonably.
B /ʌ Do you / think it'll be / born on the e/leventh, as you / said?
A /ʌ He'll be / born on the e/leventh at e/leven, as I / said. /ʌ/ / Punctually!

From 'Stress Time', *Elements of Pronunciation* by Colin Mortimer.

KEY

Stressed words

sugar = noun	prefer = verb
do = full verb (not	bit = noun
auxiliary here)	reasonably = adverb
making = verb	eleventh = adjective
comfortable = adjective	punctually = adverb
born = verb	usually = adverb
sick = adjective	recently = adverb
think = verb	said = verb

Words that carry information are stressed, i.e. nouns, adjectives, adverbs, verbs. Functional grammatical words are not usually stressed, i.e. pronouns, prepositions, auxiliary verbs, articles, quantifiers.

FOLLOW-UP

Work with more dialogues from 'Stress Time' in *Elements of Pronunciation*. Listen, repeat, and shadow read, i.e. turn the volume low and read with the tape.

Comments to the teacher

1 As a next stage, students can listen to a text or dialogue being read and mark the stresses and pauses they hear.

2 Eventually, students can also be asked to mark a text with slashes to show stress and pause marks *before* they listen. Then, they listen to the text being read, and try to hear where it differs from what they marked. They should think about the reasons for the differences. (It should be emphasized that 'different' in this context will not necessarily mean wrong.)

3 Other important aspects of English rhythm are the correct linking of words and the use of weak forms. *Elements of Pronunciation* provides practice dialogues which focus on the important details of these two areas. A tape is provided which enables students to both listen and repeat at leisure.

Speaking – the global skill

With self-access speaking activities, as with free writing activities, there is a basic problem of feedback. This is inevitable because feedback on self-access activities can only be provided when there is just one right answer or, at most, one or two possible alternatives which can be given in the key. But if a speaking activity has only one possible response then it is a form of structure drill which more properly belongs in the Grammar or Building blocks sections. It cannot be said to provide practice in the global skill of speaking. Nevertheless, it is possible to include such a section in a self-access facility if teachers and students take the wider view that self-directed *learning* is involved rather than just self-access activities that have answers.

If students are to engage in self-directed speaking activities which practise global speaking skills, they will need a room where they can speak without disturbing anyone else. Ideally, the room would be furnished like a sitting or common room – comfortable chairs around low tables – rather than like a classroom, but a classroom can, of course, be used if necessary. If it is possible to set a room aside for speaking activities, then it makes sense to store the speaking activities in that room. If your institution already has a students' common room or equivalent area, then this can be used as a 'speaking room' as well as a room to relax in. If there is no room available, then self-directed speaking packs can be loaned to students who can then make their own arrangements outside school.

It is very important that self-access speaking activities are designed to accomplish a particular task and lead to a definite outcome. Examples of such activities are:

– information which needs to be communicated (see 4.25)
– a game to be won (see 4.31)
– a problem to be solved (see 4.32).

Problem-solving and information-gap activities have the advantage of being able to give realistic feedback in the form of success or failure to complete the task. The idea of a definite outcome also gives the activity a purpose which, in the absence of a teacher, is an important motivational factor. Another important point for motivation is that the activities should be as enjoyable and entertaining as possible so that students really *want* to do them, even though they will have to do without the stimulus of overt teacher approval.

For self-access speaking activities, as with free writing activities, the preparation and training given to students is vital, and it is for this reason that this section begins with study guides.

Study guides
If they are to practise speaking on their own, students need to believe that they are engaging in useful practice when they speak to each other, even though no teacher is present to assess their performance. A study guide such as the following can be used to raise student awareness in this area (see 4.23 and 4.24).

Peer matching
In order to practise speaking, students need someone to speak to and so there needs to be some organizational framework which will allow students to match themselves with others of like mind and level. This may simply take the form of a notice displayed in the library or common room such as the one below:

Name	Class	Times available

Communication tasks
Communication tasks are game-like activities based on the information-gap principle, that is to say that in each task one person or group has information which the other person or group does not have, and only spoken communication can bridge the 'gap'.

Because students are going to use these activities on their own, clear instructions are obviously of vital importance. Careful thought also needs to be given to storage: many of the activities described in this section involve a number of 'bits and pieces', and the storage system you choose needs to take account of this. Possibly the simplest solution, and a fairly inexpensive one, is to use envelopes within pocket folders with labels on the front and on the spine. Many of these activities call for some kind of screen between students, and folders can be useful in this respect as well. It is a good idea to laminate the instructions and secure them to the *outside* of the folder so that students can discover what the activity involves and whether it appeals or not without taking out all the contents.

The fact that many of the activities do contain bits and pieces also poses a maintenance problem. Inevitably, some of the bits will go missing or be misfiled, and so someone needs to be responsible for regularly checking the folders, or, better still, provide a tray where students can place defective folders.

Most communication tasks can be adapted for use at a number of levels, from fairly elementary students right up to advanced level. The following four parameters can be manipulated to increase or decrease the linguistic difficulty of the activity:

1 Information sharing
The degree to which information is shared affects the linguistic complexity an activity is likely to produce (cf Littlewood *Communicative Language Teaching*). If students can just ask 'Yes/No' questions, not much information will be shared and the language of the activity will not get very complex. If students can ask all kinds of questions, and offer unlimited help and information to each other, then the language produced will, of course, be much more valid and complicated (see 4.25, 4.26, 4.27, and 4.28).

2 Degree of similarity
In activities where students have to discover similarities e.g. 4.26, or differences, e.g. 4.28, the less obvious the differences, the more difficult the activity will be. So that, for example, 4.26 would be more difficult if the radio were on a chair in every picture, because the pictures would then be more similar and thus more difficult to distinguish.

3 Degree of complexity
Activities which involve students in describing visuals, e.g. 4.27, will be more difficult if the visual is complex. The easiest visuals to describe will involve only a few elements whose relation to one another is fairly simple. Similarly, in activities where students have to narrate a story, e.g. 4.29, stories with few characters or elements with a simple chain of cause and effect will be easiest. If there is more than one character in the story, the more easily distinguishable they are, (i.e. different sexes, ages, etc.) the easier the activity will be.

4 Degree of abstractness
The more concrete the elements and relations in an activity are, the easier it will be, so that in 4.27, for example, abstract drawings are more difficult to describe than representations of people, animals,

buildings, simple objects, etc. Similarly, in 4.29, concrete events are easier to narrate than abstract feelings and moods.

Another way of making communication tasks less demanding and also of making them more obviously instructive in the eyes of students, is to provide models of useful or suitable language which students can consult or imitate if they wish. This can simply be a vocabulary list or a list of useful phrases (see 4.30). Another possibility for more advanced students is to tape native speakers performing the communication task, playing the game, etc. This tape can then be included in the folder as one possible model, although it must be made clear to the students that such a tape does not constitute the 'right' answer. Such tapes can serve a dual purpose in that they can also be included in the Listening section as an activity in which students are asked to describe or categorize the task or game, etc. More advanced students can be requested to write down the rules of the game or the instructions for the task. You will also need to indicate on the activity the number of people it is designed for, as this may vary from activity to activity.

4.23 Speaking for real

CLASSIFICATION   S.SG/1 = Speaking. Study guide/1

LEVEL   Intermediate to Advanced

AGE   Young adult/adult

ACTIVITY TYPE   Study guide

STUDY GUIDE   How can you improve your spoken English? Is it possible to improve your speaking outside the classroom without the help of a teacher? Think about the following questions to help you decide:

1 When people speak to one another in the real world do they usually communicate in large groups of ten or more or do they usually communicate in small groups of two or three?

2 When you have to speak English outside a classroom, will there be someone listening for your mistakes and correcting you?

3 In real-life communication which is more important: complete grammatical accuracy or the ability to get a message across?

4 If, while you are speaking English to someone in a real-life situation, you suddenly need a word but you do not know the English for it, what sort of things can you do to make yourself understood? Does solving this kind of problem teach you anything?

5 Can you learn to ride a bicycle without actually riding, or learn to swim without actually swimming? And what does this question have to do with learning a language?

6 Is there any point in practising speaking without a teacher to listen to you and correct you? If your answer to this question is 'No', how many minutes a week do you manage to spend speaking with a teacher listening to you?

7 When you have to speak English outside a classroom, will you only speak to people whose native language is English, or do you think you will have to communicate in English with people who are not native speakers?

8 If you listened to a recording of yourself speaking English do you think you would hear any mistakes and, if so, do you think you could correct them. Would you learn anything from the experience?

COMMENTARY

1 When people communicate it is usually in small groups of two or three. Natural communication in a large group such as a whole class is not easy, especially for shy people or anyone anxious about their spoken English.

2 Once you are outside the classroom you are on your own. Your teacher will not be there to correct your mistakes.

3 Grammatical accuracy is important, but accuracy is a means to an end. For most people in most situations getting a message across is more important than speaking with complete grammatical accuracy. (Of course, both together is great!)

4 People have various strategies they use when they do not know a word in a foreign language: gesture and mime, drawing pictures, using another word, explaining the word, e.g. 'a little thing – medicine – you eat to stop pain' for 'analgesic tablet'. People can become very good at using these strategies with practice.

5 Learning to speak a language is like learning to ride a bicycle or learning to swim, inasmuch as the only way you can really learn to do it is by doing it!

6 Any practice you can get in speaking English is useful whether or not a teacher is listening to you. There is too little lesson time and too many students in a class for a teacher to have the time to listen to you speak for long enough to give you adequate practice.

7 Speaking English to other people who speak it as a foreign language is probably very good practice for the way you will most often use English in your life. That is to say the most common use of English around the world is as a lingua franca, a common language which people whose native language tongue is not English, use to communicate with one another.

8 There is a lot of useful work you can do on your speaking without a teacher, if you record yourself speaking with another student, and then listen critically to what you have said.

4.24 Improving your spoken English

CLASSIFICATION   S.SG/2 = Speaking. Study guide/2

LEVEL   **Intermediate to Advanced**

AGE   **Adolescent upwards**

ACTIVITY TYPE   **Study guide**

STUDY GUIDE   This study guide gives you some ideas for improving your speaking by working on your own without a teacher.

1 Practise speaking English outside the classroom. Find someone to speak to (see 2 below) and something to talk about (see 3 below) and seize every opportunity to speak English.

2 If you can find a native-speaker of English to practise on, then that is fine. But if not, you should not give up. Find a partner or a group of people who are learning English, who are at about the same level as you and who want to practise speaking. Then organize a regular time together when you can meet and speak English. Try and arrange for a notice to be put up in a central place, a common room or library, on which people who wanted to practise speaking English could sign their names and say when they were available.

3 Make sure you have a definite plan in mind for each session when you meet with others to practise speaking. Here are some suggestions:
– do a communication task (look for activities with the classification S.CT/. . .)
– play a game (look for activities with the classification S.GA/. . .)
– solve a problem together (look for activities with the classification S.PS/. . .)
– find a play to read together.

Do not forget that the whole purpose of meeting is to talk English so make sure that *all* discussion before, during, and after the activity is in English.

4 If you really cannot find someone else to practise with, practise on your own. Find materials such as short stories, poems or plays that you can read aloud to practise pronunciation and expression. Find yourself a pen-friend but instead of always writing, try exchanging 'spoken letters' on cassettes.

5 Do try to record yourself whenever possible when you speak (audio recording or video recording, depending on resources available). When you have finished speaking, listen carefully to the tape. What was good? What was bad? Make notes about things to pay attention to in future. If you have the patience, repeat the activity and try to improve your performance.

4.25 Identify the pair

CLASSIFICATION	S.CT/1 = Speaking. Communication task/1
LEVEL	**Elementary to Lower intermediate**
AGE	**All**
ACTIVITY TYPE	**Communication task**
NUMBER OF SPEAKERS	**Two – A and B**
AIM	To practise spoken communication: giving and asking for information.
INSTRUCTIONS FOR A	**1** In the folder you will find several pictures and an envelope. Do not open the envelope
	2 Give the envelope to **B**.
	3 Your partner has a picture that is identical to one of your pictures.
	4 Ask **B** as many questions as you need to until you know which of your pictures is identical to **B**'s.
	5 Show your pictures to **B** and discuss any language difficulties.

A's PICTURES

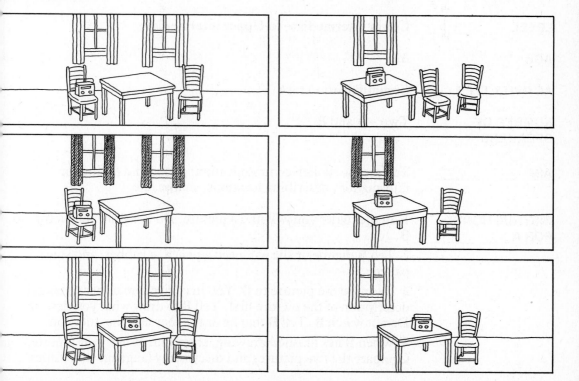

B's PICTURE

Comments to the teacher
Any set of pictures which are similar to each other can be used.
Cartoon strips are a good source for this activity or simple drawings
can be used if there is someone at hand willing and able to produce
them.

4.26 Describe and draw

CLASSIFICATION	S.CT/2 = Speaking. Communication task/2
LEVEL	**Lower intermediate to Upper intermediate**
AGE	**All**
ACTIVITY TYPE	**Communication task**
NUMBER OF SPEAKERS	**Two – A and B**
AIM	To practise spoken communication: giving and asking for information; describing locations, shapes, etc.
INSTRUCTIONS FOR A	1 In the folder you will find a picture. Do not show the picture to **B**. 2 Tell **B** that he or she will need a pencil, a rubber, and some paper. 3 Describe the picture to **B**. You may give him or her a general description of the picture first. Tell **B** to draw what you describe. Do not watch **B**. Tell **B** that he or she may ask you questions. 4 When **B** has finished drawing, show him or her your picture. Compare the two pictures and discuss any language difficulties.

Comments to the teacher

As stated above, abstract subjects are more difficult to speak about and describe than concrete ones. If you wish to make this activity really difficult, use an abstract geometric drawing such as the one below:

4.27 Describe and arrange

CLASSIFICATION	S.CT/3 = Speaking. Communication task/3
LEVEL	Lower intermediate to Upper intermediate
AGE	Junior/adolescent
ACTIVITY TYPE	Communication task
NUMBER OF SPEAKERS	Two – A and B
AIM	To practise spoken communication: giving and asking for information; describing actions and locations.

INSTRUCTIONS FOR A

1 In this folder you will find a picture. Do not show it to **B**.

You will also find an envelope containing a blank version of your picture and sixteen small pictures. Pass the envelope to **B** without looking at it.

2 Your picture consists of **B**'s small pictures arranged in order. Hide your picture from **B**. Tell **B** how to arrange his or her pictures in the same way. Tell **B** that he or she may ask you questions.

3 When **B** has finished arranging his or her pictures, show him or her your picture. Compare the two arrangements and discuss any language difficulties.

A's PICTURE

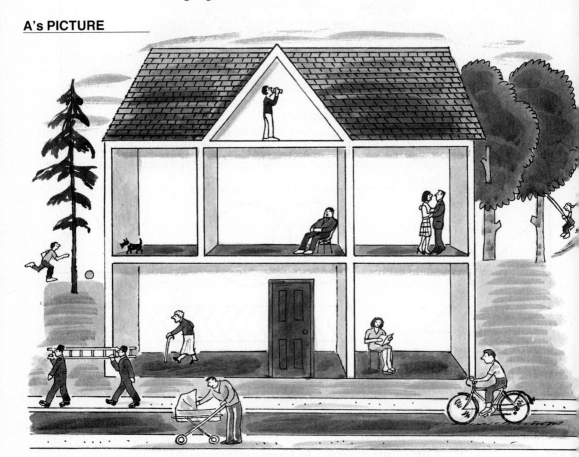

B's PICTURES

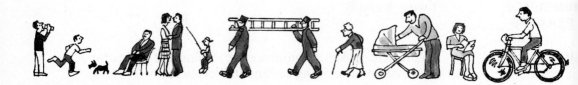

Comments to the teacher

1 The background scene and small pictures used in the example above are similar to those which can be found in the visual aids pack: Holden *Materials for Language Teaching – Interaction Package A*. This pack also contains a variety of other background scenes you could use such as 'The countryside', 'The town', and 'The room', and there are numerous small pictures which go with each scene.

2 If commercially-produced materials are not available, then this activity can be prepared with drawings or magazine pictures. You need two copies of the magazine. Background scenes are not absolutely necessary. You could provide students A and B with two sets of ten identical pictures of people, buildings, or objects, cut out from the magazines. Student B arranges his or her pictures secretly, and then describes to Student A how to arrange them in the same way.

4.28 Find the difference

CLASSIFICATION	S.CT/4 = Speaking. Communication task/4
LEVEL	Intermediate to Advanced
AGE	All
ACTIVITY TYPE	Communication task
NUMBER OF SPEAKERS	Two – A and B
AIM	To practise spoken communication: giving and asking for information, and describing a scene.
INSTRUCTIONS FOR A	1 In this folder you will find two envelopes. Take one and give the other to **B**.

2 There is a picture in each envelope. Do not show your picture to **B**.

3 Your picture is similar to that of **B**, but there are some differences. Talk to one another until you find five differences.

4 When you have found the five differences, show your pictures to one another and compare them. Try to find more differences.

A's PICTURE

B's PICTURE

Comments to the teacher

1 Other 'find-the-difference' pictures can be found as competitions in newspapers, magazines, or children's comics. Also useful for this activity are the contrast pictures used in some advertisements such as the 'before and after the diet' type, or the 'which couple has made adequate provision for retirement?' type. More examples of such pictures can be found in Olsen *Look Again Pictures*, and Bell *In Focus – A Visual Resource Book for the EFL Teacher*.

2 As a variation, the pictures can be adapted for use with more than two people by using 'Tipp-Ex' liquid and a black pen to alter a few more details. This then becomes a very demanding activity, especially if students are not told how many differences there are.

4.29 Tell the story

CLASSIFICATION S.CT/5 = Speaking. Communication/5

LEVEL Intermediate to Advanced

AGE Adolescent upwards

ACTIVITY TYPE Communication task

NUMBER OF SPEAKERS Four students

AIM To practise spoken communication: giving and asking for information, describing, narrating.

INSTRUCTIONS **Note**: do not open the envelope marked 'X'.

1 Each student takes an envelope. Inside the envelope there is a picture. Look at the picture but do not show it to any of the other students.

2 Take it in turns to describe your pictures.

3 Decide together which picture comes first, which second, etc. in order to make a story.

4 Tell the story in the past tense, each person relating that part of the story which goes with his or her picture.

5 Now place your pictures in order on the table and check your answer with the solution in the envelope marked 'X'.

THE PICTURES

Comments to the teacher

1 For this activity you need to find some old picture composition books that are no longer needed. Two copies of each picture story are necessary: one is cut up and each piece of picture put into a separate envelope, while the other is kept intact and put into an envelope marked with an 'X'. There must be as many students as there are pictures.

2 Useful sources for communication activities which can be adapted for self-directed speaking are *Beginning Composition through Pictures, Composition through Pictures,* Hadfield *Harraps Communication Games,* Hadfield *Advanced Communication Games,* some activities Klippel *Keep Talking,* and Watcyn-Jones *Pairwork.* Ideas for such activities are also often found in teachers' magazines such as *Modern English Teacher* and *Practical English Teacher.*

Games

Self-access games are very popular with students and excellent for encouraging them to speak English to one another while playing. The competitive ingredient present in all games gives the activity purpose, while motivation is provided by the 'fun' aspect. It is a good idea to provide a study guide for students to work through before they play any of the games, in order to give them expressions in English which they can use while playing the game (see 4.30 and 4.31).

EFL games

Games for Pairwork (Astrop and Byrne): a small book of board games for two players with clear instructions. Dice and counters need to be supplied.

It's Your Turn (Byrne): a large format book of board-like games, most games being played on a two-page spread. Dice and counters need to be supplied.

Jabberwocky (Wakeman): basically a word game. Players have to combine words and word-endings to create sentences. The instructions will need simplifying.

'The Bus Game' and 'The Desert Island Game' from *Materials for Language Teaching – Interaction Package B* (Holden): these games need putting together into packs with clear self-access instructions. Players have to argue their case and other players may challenge them. Those who can argue most convincingly win.

Non-EFL games

Many commercially-produced non-EFL games can usefully be included in the Speaking section. Games such as chess or draughts are not, however, suitable for our purposes since it is possible to play them almost in silence. In contrast, games like 'Happy Families' (OXFAM produce a version with families from all over the world), 'Cluedo' (Waddingtons) – a murder detection game; 'Diplomacy' (Waddingtons) – a game requiring diplomatic negotiation in forming alliances and betraying them – all of these require a lot of verbal communication.

4.30 Language for games

CLASSIFICATION	S.GA/1 = Speaking. Games/1
LEVEL	Lower intermediate to Upper intermediate
AGE	Adolescent/young adult
ACTIVITY TYPE	Study guide
AIM	To teach some phrases which you might need when playing a game in English.
INSTRUCTIONS	Here are some useful phrases for playing games. Make sure you know what they all mean, use a dictionary if necessary. Try and use some of the phrases each time you play a game, and remember: speak English all the time!

STUDY GUIDE

Before you start

How do you play the game?
Read out the rules.
Where's the dice?
Who goes first?
How many counters do we need?
Shall I keep score?
Will you be banker?

While you are playing

Whose turn is it?
Come on! It's your turn.

Don't cheat!
What's the score?
Who's winning?
It's not fair! Just my luck!
Move your counter on six places.

At the end

Who's won?
Well done!
Better luck next time.
Help me put the game away.
Shall we play again tomorrow?

4.31 Out of the hat

CLASSIFICATION	S.GA/2 = Speaking.Games/2
LEVEL	Intermediate to Advanced
AGE	Young adult/adult
ACTIVITY TYPE	Game
NUMBER OF SPEAKERS	Two to six players
EQUIPMENT	A cassette recorder and a blank cassette for recording (desirable but not essential).

AIM

To practise speaking English while enjoying playing a game.

INSTRUCTIONS

1 In the envelope marked 'X' are a number of pieces of paper folded over. Each piece of paper is folded over so that you cannot see what is written on it. Put the pieces of paper into a hat or a box, but make sure you do not look at what is written on them.

2 Each piece of paper has a subject written on it such as 'My favourite hobby'. Each player in turn picks a piece of paper out of the hat and looks at it for no longer than ten seconds. The player talks for two minutes on the subject without stopping. (It is a good idea to record these talks so you can listen to yourself afterwards.)

Comments to the teacher

1 The following is a list of suggested subjects which the students could be asked to talk about:

An embarrassing moment
The worst/best holiday I've ever had
Childhood fears
Clothes – what they tell you about the wearer
Superstitions
English food
Keeping fit
The twenty-first century
The USA
My type of music
What I like doing in my spare time

2 The example given is an idea from *101 Word Games*, by G McCallum. The subjects need to be written out on separate pieces of paper and the paper folded over with the writing inside. Put all the pieces of paper into an envelope and mark it with an 'X'. (As a variation on this game, it can be suggested to the students that they provide the subjects.)

3 There are many commercially-produced games, EFL and non-EFL, which make a useful addition to the Speaking section. A selection is described on page 144.

Problem solving with an information gap

Problem-solving activities with an in-built information gap require students to exchange information so that they can solve a problem.

4.32 Dangerous island

CLASSIFICATION	S.PS/1 = Speaking. Problem solving/1
LEVEL	**Intermediate to Advanced**
AGE	**Adolescent/young adult**
ACTIVITY TYPE	**Problem solving**
NUMBER OF SPEAKERS	**Two students**
AIM	To exchange information and solve a problem co-operatively by speaking.
PREPARATION	Do not open the folder until you have read the instructions.
INSTRUCTIONS FOR A	**1** Your map is in the envelope marked 'A'. Do not show your map to **B**.

2 You are at Camp X. **B** is at Camp Y and must find the way to you at Camp X. You can talk by radio. You both have a map of the island but be careful! Your maps are slightly different . Neither of you has all the information you need. Your task is to guide **B** and find a safe route for him or her over to Camp X.

3 A map showing the solution is in the envelope marked 'X'. Do not look at it until you have finished the activity.

MAP FOR A

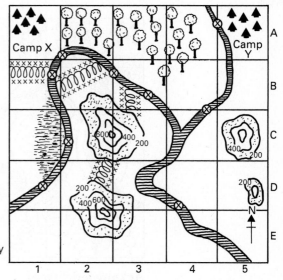

Symbol		Description
	= *Forest*	Do not enter this area. It is mined and contains dangerous animals.
	= *Swamp*	Do not cross this area. It is impassable to men and vehicles
	= *Hill*	Do not cross this area. It is heavily guarded by the enemy.
	= *Barbed Wire Barricades and Electric Fences*	Avoid these obstacles.
	= *Ford*	The rivers may be crossed by men and vehicles only at these places.

INSTRUCTIONS FOR B

1 Your map is in the envelope marked 'B'. Do not show your map to **A**.

2 You are at Camp Y. **A** is at Camp X and you must find the way to meet him or her at Camp X. You can talk by radio. You both have a map of the island but be careful! Your maps are slightly different. Neither of you has all the information you need. Your task is to find a safe route to Camp X. **A** will help you.

3 A map showing the solution is in the envelope marked 'X'. Do not look at it until you have finished the activity.

MAP FOR B

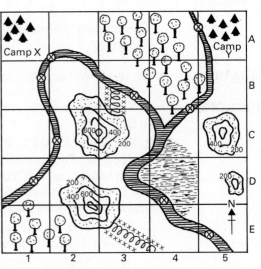

🌳 🌳	= *Forest*	Do not enter this area. It is mined and contains dangerous animals.
≈≈≈	= *Swamp*	Do not cross this area. It is impassable to men and vehicles
🗻	= *Hill*	Do not cross this area. It is heavily guarded by the enemy.
ⱷⱷⱷⱷ	= *Barbed Wire Barricades and Electric Fences*	Avoid these obstacles.
⊗	= *Ford*	The rivers may be crossed by men and vehicles only at these places.

KEY

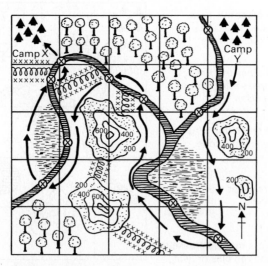

Acknowledgement

The above example is an idea taken from *Communicative Language Teaching*, by William Littlewood (copyright David Cobb).

4.33 A treasure hunt

CLASSIFICATION	S.PS/2 = Speaking. Problem solving/2
LEVEL	Upper intermediate to Advanced
AGE	Adolescent/young adult
ACTIVITY TYPE	Problem solving
NUMBER OF SPEAKERS	Three students
AIM	To exchange information and solve a problem co-operatively by speaking.
PREPARATION	People have always dreamed of finding buried treasure. It is not only the hope of finding gold and precious stones which excites them but the search itself – following the clues and piecing together the information. Some people seem to enjoy hiding treasure as much as others enjoy seeking it.

1 Read the newspaper report. What did the millionaire bury? Did he leave any clues?

Eccentric Millionaire Buries Treasure

was confirmed by lawyers yesterday that eccentric millionaire Harry Evans who died last month had buried the priceless Hadley jewel. They said that Mr Evans, who had no family himself, felt that the jewel from his private collection should go to 'someone who wanted it enough to search for it'. He left a number of verses as clues to the whereabouts of the buried treasure. The Hadley jewel consists of a gold chain and pendant which contains two miniature portraits. Apparently Mr Evans buried the piece in a water-proof container somewhere beyond the range of metal detectors.

Experts described the piece yesterday as 'unique' and expressed anxiety for its safety.

STAGE 1

1 **A, B,** and **C** should work by themselves at this stage. **A** read text 1, **B** read text 2, and **C** read text 3 below.

Here are some of the clues Harry Evans left:

Whether it rains or whether it shines
These are the last of the precious lines.

Now you must look for the leaves of the vine
Because what you are seeking is buried under time.

Here is an extract from *A Guide to Country Walks*: The visitor can leave his car at Ashton picnic area. He can then follow the rough path south past the ruins of an old castle on his right. This is known as Alfred's castle. The grassy hill commands a fine view of the valley below. Little remains of the castle now because the stone was taken to build the stately house set in the magnificent park that can be seen in the village to the south west. This is Hadley Hall. The hall is elegant and has been described as a perfect doll's house. It stands with its west facade looking onto the river while the east faces the village. The visitor can continue on this path, passing on his left the curious Black Mouse stone, and then down into the village emerging between cottages in the village street. Refreshments can be had at the local inn, the Black Lion, an Elizabethan building dated 1590. Return to Ashton car park by the main road or retrace your footsteps along the path.

Here are some of the clues Harry Evans left:

> Whether it rains or whether it shines
> This is the middle of the precious lines.

> If you come early or if you come late,
> Go under the three birds that sit on the gate.

Here is an extract from *A Visitor's Guide to the Emm Valley*: As you enter the village of Harbury on the B3300 road you see first the village pond which lies beside the old church of St. Mary. Opposite the church is one of the finest Elizabethan inns in the country. Don't miss the walled garden which reaches down to the river. If the sun is shining you can check your watch with the time shown by the old sundial in the centre of the garden. Made in local stone in 1760 the top of the sundial has a fine brass plate where the hours are clearly written and the surrounding metal is decorated with grapes and vine leaves. The highlight of the village is the Earl of Swinley's stately home.

Here are some of the clues Harry Evans left:

> Whether it rains or whether it shines
> These are the first of the precious lines.

> If you are short or if you are tall
> From Alfred's hill you can see it all.

> Walk quickly south past the old doll's house,
> Seek a black lion, not a black mouse.

Here is an extract from *The Country Lover's Guide to Villages*: The River Emm winds its way through the charming village of Harbury. Harbury has more than its fair share of places of historical interest: a stately home, a fine church and a village pub. However, perhaps the oldest building in the village is in some ways the most interesting. As you come into Harbury from the south, the village pond is on your right and a little further on to your left you will see some high walls and an old gateway built straight onto the village street. This is all that remains of the old abbey and the walls enclose a walled flower garden. The garden and the walls adjoin the old village inn and the walls run round the corner down a narrow lane and north-west to the river. The gateway itself has been dated at about 1295 although the walls may be earlier. The visitor who looks up will see an interesting stone carving of a shield above the arch of the gate. On the shield can be seen three birds carved in white stone. Nothing is left of the abbey itself.

2 You have only *some* of the clues that Harry Evans left – read yours carefully. Make a careful copy of your clue (the lines that rhyme at the top of the reading text).

3 Name as many things as you can on the map below.

4 In your notebook make short notes about the buildings and monuments you have marked on the map.

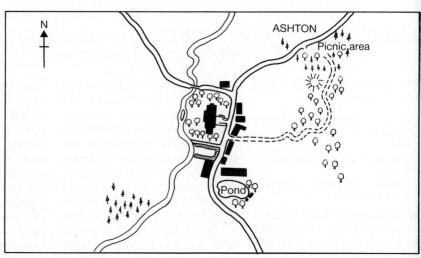

A, B, and, **C** form a discussion group. Put away your texts now. You can refer only to your map, your notebook, and your clue.

1 Each student finds out what the other two students have named on their maps. Do this by means of speaking only. Do not show the maps to each other.

2 Each student finds out about the buildings and monuments of the other two students. Do this by means of speaking only. Do not show your notebooks to each other.

3 Put all your clues together in the right order. Which clue is the first? Which the second, and which the third?

4 Decide together where the Hadley Jewel is buried. Mark the exact spot on the map.

5 Check the key to see if you are right.

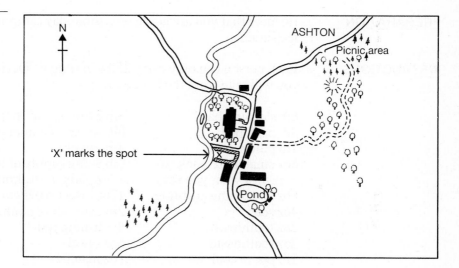

Comments to the teacher
The above example is an idea taken from *Reading Links* by Marion Geddes and Gill Sturtridge. This material was not designed to be used by students on their own, but it can be adapted for three participants by giving step by step instructions, as has been done above. The three texts should be put into separate envelopes labelled 'Text 1', 'Text 2', and 'Text 3'. The key should be put into an envelope and labelled as 'Key' with a warning not to open the envelope before reading the instructions and solving the problem. An abundant supply of blank maps and tables is necessary.

Problem solving with no information gap

Students can be given realistic problems such as they might face in real life and then their task is to co-operate in trying to find a good solution by means of discussion and negotiation.

4.34 The camping trip

CLASSIFICATION   S.PS/3 = Speaking. Problem solving/3

LEVEL   Lower intermediate to Intermediate

AGE   Adolescent/adult

ACTIVITY TYPE   Problem solving

NUMBER OF SPEAKERS   Two to six students

AIM   To exchange information and solve a problem co-operatively by speaking.

PREPARATION   Imagine that you are going on a three-day camping trip in the mountains.

INSTRUCTIONS   Each person can only carry 25lbs in weight. Decide together what you will take from the list below:

6lb sleeping bag	3lb extra pair of shoes
3lb pack bag	6lb water container (full of water)
1lb pillow	4lb camera
6oz small note book (to record what you see)	6lb 3-day supply of food
	12oz plate, fork, knife, spoon
8oz swimming costume	12oz insect repellent
4oz soap	2lb extra set of clothing
2oz toothbrush	3lb fishing rod
2oz toothpaste	6oz towel
1lb pot to cook in	1oz matches
1lb flashlight	1lb rain jacket

Comments to the teacher

1 The example above is an idea taken from *Developing Communicative Competence – Interaction Activities in English as a Second Language*, by J C Kettering.

2 Other examples of real-life type problems include:
– Plan the redecoration or refurnishing of a room with a list of possible purchases to choose from (perhaps a real catalogue) but with a limit on the amount of money that can be spent
– Plan an itinerary on the basis of information on transport and timetables, possible sights to visit with visiting times and entry fees, a map, etc.
– Useful sources for other problem-solving activities are Maley an Grellet *Mind Matters* and Ladousse *Speaking Personally*.

5 Building blocks

This section focuses on grammar, vocabulary, and social language (here meaning useful set phrases for certain stock situations). To a large extent these can be considered the building blocks of language, where the accent is on accuracy. Grammar and vocabulary work give the student an opportunity to take a temporary step back from the hurly-burly of real-time interaction in order to investigate and practise a discrete area of the language at his or her own pace. This enables students to reflect consciously on the language in a way that they cannot when they are actually engaged in communication.

Needless to say, this particular house cannot be built merely by learning about the individual bricks, and students must be made aware of the fact that accuracy training *alone* will not produce the desired effects of improved language production and/or comprehension. In conjunction with global skill practice, however, occasional concentration on grammar and vocabulary will contribute much towards improved performance all round, as a support to more authentic communication in the language, not as a substitute for it.

Grammar

This area tends to be very popular for self-access work, reflecting the fact that many students believe that grammar is what language learning is really all about. In adults, this can be partly due to their language learning experience at school, where grammar learning and accuracy may have received great emphasis compared with fluency activities. In part, though, it can be seen as evidence of a natural human inclination to analyse and organize experience.

The fact that some students feel that grammar practice is 'good' for them does not remove the necessity for making practice material as engaging as possible. Grammar can be a 'dry' subject for private study and students' motivation needs to be maintained. The liberal use of picture prompts, together with challenging tasks and intriguing situations can go a long way to sweetening the pill.

In the Grammar and Vocabulary sections there is usually a need for a more comprehensive classification system than in the other sections of the self-access facility. Here the 'Activity type' assumes less importance, as it is the particular 'Language focus' that students will want to search for.

The Grammar section will need to be divided up into sub-categories such as 'Verb phrase', 'Noun phrase', etc. This is, however, still too broad to be really useful to students, and so there is a need for at least one further level of sub-classification. Below is an example of how a grammar section could be organized and classified:

G.VP Verb phrase
G.VP1 Time/tenses
G.VP2 Modals/conditionals
G.VP3 Question forms/short answers
G.VP4 Passive/active/imperative moods (G.VP4/1 would be the first item in this sub-section)

G.NP Noun phrase
G.NP1 Countable/uncountable/quantifiers
G.NP2 Articles
G.NP3 Pronouns: personal/possessive/demonstrative/relative
G.NP4 Apostrophe 's' (G.NP4/1 would be the first item in this sub-section)

G.ADJ Adjectives
G.ADJ1 Comparatives/superlatives
G.ADJ2 Word order
G.ADJ3 Possessive adjectives
G.ADJ4 Demonstrative adjectives (G.ADJ4/1 would be the first item in this sub-section)

G.ADV Adverbs
G.ADV1 Comparatives/superlatives
G.ADV2 Word order
G.ADV3 Formation from adjectives (including irregulars)
(G.ADV3/1 would be the first item in this sub-section)

G.PREP Prepositions
G.PREP1 Simple meaning relationships
G.PREP2 Complex meaning relationships (G.PREP2/1 would be the first item in this sub-section)

Much more complex organizations and finer classification systems than this one are possible, of course, and the above is intended merely as an example of what a system could look like. Schools and colleges often develop their own system in response to local needs.

Learner training in the use of the system is essential. Even a simple organization like the one above can be daunting for those who are not familiar with the terminology, and it may be necessary to help further by, for example:

- simplifying terminology, e.g *the/a/an* instead of 'Articles'
- prominently displaying a reference sheet which highlights examples of the item concerned in sample phrases or sentences, e.g. 'Prepositions' – *on* the table, *in* the box (see D Bolton, M Oscarson & L Peterson *Basic Working Grammar* for an example of such a list)
- providing an index of key words which will direct students to the section they need, e.g. *this* book – see Demonstrative adjectives.

The activities in this section are organized and classified in accordance with the above example system, although there is not an activity for each sub-section.

5.1 Nicola's room

CLASSIFICATION   G.VP1/1 = Grammar. Verb phrase. Time/tenses/1

LANGUAGE FOCUS   **Present simple**: habitual action

LEVEL   **Elementary**

AGE   **Adolescent/young adult**

ACTIVITY TYPE   **Problem solving and practice activity**

AIM   To give you practice in using the present simple tense to describe how someone lives.

PREPARATION   In order to do this activity you will need to have learnt about the present simple tense and how to use it to talk about habitual action. If you do not understand this or if you are not quite sure whether you have learnt it or not, see . . . (reference to a section in a grammar book, e.g. M Swan *Basic English Usage*, sections 261.1 and 261.2 or D Bolton, M Oscarson & L Peterson *Basic Working Grammar*, sections 64–66, or to a specially in-house prepared study guide).

INSTRUCTIONS   1 You do not know Nicola, but you can write a lot about her just by looking at her room. For example:
Nicola drives a car.
Nicola doesn't smoke.

2 Now write eight sentences about Nicola using these verbs: *play, listen to, read, wear, drink, eat, watch, take.*

KEY	She *plays* the guitar.
	She *listens* to records / classical music.
	She *reads* magazines.
	She *wears* jeans.
	She *drinks* coffee.
	She *eats* spaghetti.
	She *watches* television / TV.
	She *takes* photographs / photos.

FOLLOW-UP   If you made mistakes in the verbs above, see (reference to study guide).

Comments to the teacher

1 The example above is an idea from *Play Games with English* (Book 1) by Colin Granger & John Plumb.

2 Specially drawn scenes can provide practice for many different tenses: in one picture lots of people may be *going to* do things, or may be actually *doing* them. Another kind of scene can show lots of things people *have done*, e.g. an untidy room after a party, or a room after a robbery. It is important to contextualize the activity.

5.2 A perfect evening?

CLASSIFICATION	**G.VP1/2 = Grammar. Verb phrase. Time/tenses/2**
LANGUAGE FOCUS	**Past simple**: for narration
LEVEL	**Lower intermediate**
AGE	**Young adult/adult**
ACTIVITY TYPE	**Problem solving and practice activity**
AIM	To give you practice in using the past simple tense to tell a story.
PREPARATION	In order to do this exercise you need to know how to form the past simple tense. If you do not know this, or if you just want to check, see (reference to grammar book, e.g. J Eastwood & R Mackin, *A Basic English Grammar*, or relevant study guide).
INSTRUCTIONS	1 Can you tell the story of Jack's evening? On a separate piece of paper, write the story. Put the verbs into the past tense and write in proper sentences. Use words from the list above the pictures (some words you an use more than once).
	2 Be careful! The pictures are in the wrong order.
	3 Start like this: *Jack **arrived** home and **went** into the house.*

TASK SHEET

see a letter from his wife   In bed, *feel*   *open* a bottle of champagne to celebrate   *arrive* home and go into the house   *jump* for joy

get ready for bed   *read* the letter – *learn* he is alone,   *begin* to cry   *have* a meal

KEY

Jack arrived home and went into the house. He saw a letter from his wife. When Jack read the letter and learnt he was alone, he jumped for joy. He opened a bottle of champagne to celebrate and then he had a meal. Later he got ready for bed. In bed, he felt sad and began to cry.

Comments to the teacher

1 The example above is an idea from *1000 Pictures for Language Teachers to Copy* by Andrew Wright.

2 As a variation for more advanced students, supply only the infinitive verb forms in a list.

5.3 Missing person

CLASSIFICATION

G.VP2/1 = Grammar. Verb prhase. Modals/1

LANGUAGE FOCUS

Modal verbs: speculating and making deductions about the past

LEVEL

Intermediate to Upper intermediate

AGE

Young adult/adult

ACTIVITY TYPE

Problem solving and practice activity

AIM

To give you practice in using modal verbs to speculate and make deductions about the present and the past, e.g. *must be, must have, can't be, can't have, might be, might have, could be, could have.*

PREPARATION

To do this activity you need to know how to use modal verbs to express possibilities, probabilities, and near certainties about past events. If you have forgotten how to do this or if you want to check, see (reference to grammar book, e.g. J Eastwood & R Mackin, *A Basic English Grammar*, or relevant study guide).

INSTRUCTIONS 1

1 On Task sheet 1 read the background introduction and look at the list.

2 Using one of the verbs given, write down your conclusions about the tenant's life – one conclusion per item on the list.

3 Check your answers in Key 1.

4 Go on to Task sheet 2.

ASK SHEET 1   You are a landlord or landlady and one of your tenants has not paid her rent this week. You have not heard her in her room for two days and you are rather worried as she did not tell you she was going to be away. You decide to go into her room to see if you can get any clues to her whereabouts. Being a rather nosy person, you also take the opportunity to find out a bit more about your tenant! Here is a list of things you found:

1 A student card.

2 A lot of books about economics.

3 Several empty packets of cigarettes and an ashtray full of cigarette ends.

4 A packet of love letters tied up with pink ribbon.

5 A photograph of a smiling young man on a Mediterranean beach.

6 A 'Teach Yourself Greek' book.

7 A half-packed suitcase.

For each item on the list above, write a sentence with your conclusion. The first one has been done for you.

1 *She must be a student.*

Use these verbs (with *not* if necessary): *may, might, could, must, can.*

EY 1   1 She must be a student.

2 She must be studying economics.

3 She must be a smoker / She must have smoked a lot of cigarettes.

4 She might / could be in love.

5 She might / could be in love with the man in the photograph.

6 She must be learning Greek / The man in the photograph must / might be Greek.

7 She must be going away / She might be going to Greece.

Note:
You may have some different sentences from the ones above but that does not mean they are wrong. What is wrong, however, is to use *can* to express possibility, e.g. *She can be in love* is wrong in this context.

NSTRUCTIONS 2   You search her room again a bit more thoroughly and find some more evidence. Once again, write down a sentence for each item on the list giving your conclusion about what you think has happened.

ASK SHEET 2   Here is the second list:

1 An envelope with a Greek stamp on it.

2 A fragment of a letter saying 'I'm so sorry . . . don't want to hurt you . . . don't know how to tell you . . .'

3 A ticket for a flight to Athens, today's date.

4 A passport.

5 An empty bottle of whisky.

6 An empty bottle of aspirin.

Now write your conclusions using the verbs: *must, can't, might, couldn't.*

KEY 2

1 She must have got/received a letter from her Greek boyfriend.

2 He might/must have broken off the relationship/said he didn't want to see her any more.

3 She might have flown to Athens *or* She can't/couldn't have gone/ flown to Athens because her case is still in the room.

4 She can't/couldn't have flown to Athens without her passport.

5 She might/must have been drinking/drowning her sorrows.

6 She might have taken too many aspirins/committed suicide/tried to kill herself.

Acknowledgement
The example above is adapted from an unpublished worksheet by Beverly Sedley, teacher and teacher trainer at the Bell School, Cambridge.

5.4 Cat burglar

CLASSIFICATION	G.NP2/1 = Grammar. Noun phrase. Articles/1
LANGUAGE FOCUS	Articles
LEVEL	Intermediate
AGE	Adolescent/young adult
ACTIVITY TYPE	Practice activity
AIM	To give you practice in using *the, a, an* or no article, correctly.
PREPARATION	To do this activity you need to know when to use *the* in front of nouns, when to use *a* (or *an*), and when to use no article at all.
INSTRUCTIONS	Fill in the gaps in the story with *the, a, an*, or, if necessary, do not put any article.
TASK SHEET	John lived alone in (1) . . . small house. He had (2) . . . cat to keep him company but, even so, he sometimes felt lonely. Each day he went to (3) . . . work and in (4) . . . evening he came back (5) . . . home. Nothing exciting ever happened. Then, one day, he decided

to go to (6) . . . cinema to see (7) . . . film. He left (8) . . . house, locking (9) . . . front door behind him. (10) . . . cat was asleep inside. What John didn't know, however, was that he was being watched, and about half (11) . . . hour after he left (12) . . . man came out from behind (13) . . . tree and climbed through (14) . . . open window at (15) . . . back of (16) . . . house. He went into (17) . . . sitting room and started to look for (18) . . . money in (19) . . . drawers of (20) . . . desk. (21) . . . cat was awake now and very angry with (22) . . . burglar for disturbing her. She crept silently across (23) . . . room and suddenly leapt like (24) . . . wild thing onto (25) . . . burglar's back with (26) . . . horrifying cry. (27) . . . man was terrified and ran out of (28) . . . house as fast as he could. He thought he had been attacked by (29) . . . fiend from (30) . . . hell.

KEY

1	a small house	
2	a cat	
7	a film	
12	a man	*first mention*
13	a tree	
24	a wild thing	
26	a horrifying cry	
29	a fiend	
14	an open window	*all houses have windows but this is the first mention of a window that is special, i.e. open*
18	money	*first mention, but uncountable noun*
11	half an hour	*set phrase, 'h' is not pronounced, so 'hour' begins with a vowel sound*
8	the house	
10	the cat	
16	the house	
21	the cat	*second or subsequent mention of the word*
25	the burglar's	
27	the man	
28	the house	
22	the burglar	*second or subsequent mention of the person, although first use of the word*
4	the evening	
9	the front door	
15	the back	*first mention, but unsurprising because, e.g. all days have evenings, all houses have front doors, etc.*
17	the sitting room	
19	the drawers	
20	the desk	
23	the room	

6 the cinema	*first mention, but unsurprising, i.e. not really new information, because most people have a local cinema, one that they usually go to*
3 to work **5** back home	*set phrases with no article*
30 from hell	*like 'heaven', 'hell' is used almost like a place name, therefore no article*

5.5 Medical relatives

CLASSIFICATION   G.NP3/1 = Grammar. Noun phrase. Pronouns/1

LANGUAGE FOCUS   Relative pronouns

LEVEL   Intermediate to Upper intermediate

AGE   Young adult/adult

ACTIVITY TYPE   Problem solving and practice activity

AIM   To give you practice in linking parts of sentences with correct relative pronouns.

PREPARATION   To do this activity you need to know how to introduce clauses with relative pronouns and which relative pronouns to use in which circumstances, to refer to people, things, etc. If you are unsure of this area, see (reference to grammar book, e.g. J Eastwood & R Mackin, *A Basic English Grammar*, or relevant study guide).

INSTRUCTIONS   1 Link the clauses on the left with the clauses on the right using one of the following relative pronouns: *who, where, which, whose.*

2 The clauses on the right are all jumbled up so you must work out which clause on the left goes with which clause on the right.

TASK SHEET   1 An invalid is someone _____ is in charge of a hospital ward.

2 A hospital is a place _____ there are no patients.

3 A stethoscope is a piece of equipment _____ shows the bones inside the body.

4 A diabetic is someone _____ kills bacteria.

5 An antibiotic is something _____ ensures that patients are unconscious during an operation.

6 A pathology laboratory is a place _____ people go for operations.

7 An anaesthetist is a doctor _____ is ill or has been injured.

8 A sister is someone _____ body cannot regulate the production of insulin.

9 An X-ray is something _____ the doctor uses to listen to a heart beat.

KEY

1 An invalid is someone *who* is ill or has been injured.

2 A hospital is a place *where* people go for operations.

3 A stethoscope is a piece of equipment *which* the doctor uses to listen to a heart beat.

4 A diabetic is someone *whose* body cannot regulate the production of insulin.

5 An antibiotic is something *which* kills bacteria.

6 A pathology laboratory is a place *where* there are no patients.

7 An anaesthetist is a doctor *who* ensures that patients are unconscious during an operation.

8 A sister is someone *who* is in charge of a hospital ward.

9 An X-ray is something *which* shows the bones inside the body.

5.6 Family tree

CLASSIFICATION   G.NP4/1 = Grammar. Noun phrase. Apostrophe 's'/1

LANGUAGE FOCUS   Apostrophe 's'

LEVEL   Elementary

AGE   Adolescent/adult

ACTIVITY TYPE   Practice activity

AIM   To give you practice in using *'s* and *s'* correctly.

PREPARATION   To do this activity you need to know how to use *'s* and *s'* to talk about family relationships, e.g. *John's mother*. If you are unsure about this see (reference to grammar book, e.g. J Eastwood & R Mackin, *A Basic English Grammar*, or relevant study guide).

INSTRUCTIONS   Look at the family tree and, on a separate piece of paper, write out the sentences and fill in the missing words using: *'s, s', or s*.

TASK SHEET

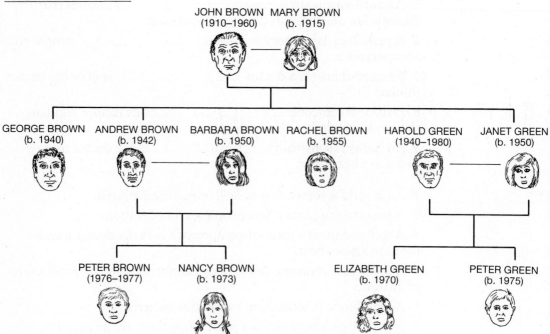

JOHN BROWN   MARY BROWN
(1910–1960)   (b. 1915)

GEORGE BROWN   ANDREW BROWN   BARBARA BROWN   RACHEL BROWN   HAROLD GREEN   JANET GREEN
(b. 1940)   (b. 1942)   (b. 1950)   (b. 1955)   (1940–1980)   (b. 1950)

PETER BROWN   NANCY BROWN   ELIZABETH GREEN   PETER GREEN
(1976–1977)   (b. 1973)   (b. 1970)   (b. 1975)

1 Andrew Brown is N . . . father.
2 The c . . . grandmother is Mary Brown.
3 Both . . . were born before 1916.
4 George is E . . . uncle.
5 Janet is Harold . . . wife.
6 N . . . baby brother died when he was one year old.
7 E . . . b . . . name is Peter.
8 Rachel has one sister and two . . . .

KEY

1 Andrew Brown is *Nancy's* father.
2 The *cousins'* grandmother is Mary Brown.
3 Both *grandparents* were born before 1916.
4 George is *Elizabeth's* uncle.
5 Janet is Harold *Green's* wife.
6 *Nancy's* baby brother died when he was one year old.
7 *Elizabeth's brother's* name is Peter.
8 Rachel has one sister and two *brothers*.

Comments to the teacher
To make this activity into a discovery task, give beginners lots of sentences about the family tree, ask them to group the three different kinds of 's', and then ask them if they can see when *'s, s',* and *s* are used.

5.7 Comparative quiz

CLASSIFICATION	**G.ADJ1/1 = Grammar. Adjectives. Comparatives/Superlatives/1**
LANGUAGE FOCUS	**Comparative adjectives**
LEVEL	**Elementary to Lower intermediate**
AGE	**Adolescent/young adult**
ACTIVITY TYPE	**Quiz and practice activity**
AIM	To give you practice in using comparative adjectives.
PREPARATION	**1** To do this activity you need to know how to make the comparative of short adjectives. If you do not know or are not sure, see (reference to grammar book or relevant study guide). **2** To do the quiz you need to know quite a lot!
INSTRUCTIONS	Compare the following. For each question write a complete sentence, on another piece of paper, for example: 1 *The Pacific Ocean is bigger than the Atlantic Ocean.*

TASK SHEET

1 PACIFIC OCEAN / ATLANTIC OCEAN — BIG

2 Parthenon / Colosseum — OLD

3 MARS / VENUS — NEAR THE SUN

4 RUSSIA / CHINA — LARGE

5 SUEZ CANAL EGYPT / PANAMA CANAL PANAMA — LONG

6 Mount Etna / mont Blanc — HIGH

7 SLOW

KEY

1 The Pacific Ocean is bigger than the Atlantic Ocean. (Pacific Ocean is 165 million km in area.)

2 The Parthenon is older than the Colosseum. (The Parthenon wa begun in 447 B.C, the Colosseum was built between A.D. 72-82.)

3 Venus is nearer the sun than Mars. (Venus is 108 million km from the sun; Mars is 228 million km.)

4 Russia is larger than China. (Russia has approximately 15% of the world's surface; China approximately 10%.)

5 The Suez Canal is longer than the Panama Canal. (The Suez Canal is 162 km long; the Panama Canal is 82 km long.)

6 Mont Blanc is higher than Mount Etna. (Mont Blanc is 4807 m high; Mount Etna 3274 m high.)

7 A snail is slower than a tortoise. (A snail travels at 0.05 km per hour; a tortoise at 0.127 km per hour.)

5.8 How?

CLASSIFICATION	**G.ADV3/1 = Grammar. Adverbs. Formation from adjectives/.**
LANGUAGE FOCUS	**Adverbs:** form
LEVEL	**Lower intermediate to Intermediate**
AGE	**Adolescent/young adult**
ACTIVITY TYPE	**Practice activity**
AIM	To give you practice in using adverbs correctly.
PREPARATION	To do this activity you need to know how to form adverbs from adjectives, and you need to know some common irregular adverbs. If you need to check on these see, for example, J Eastwood & J Mackin, *A Basic English Grammar*.
INSTRUCTIONS	On a separate piece of paper, write out and complete the sentences below with a suitable adverb each time.

TASK SHEET

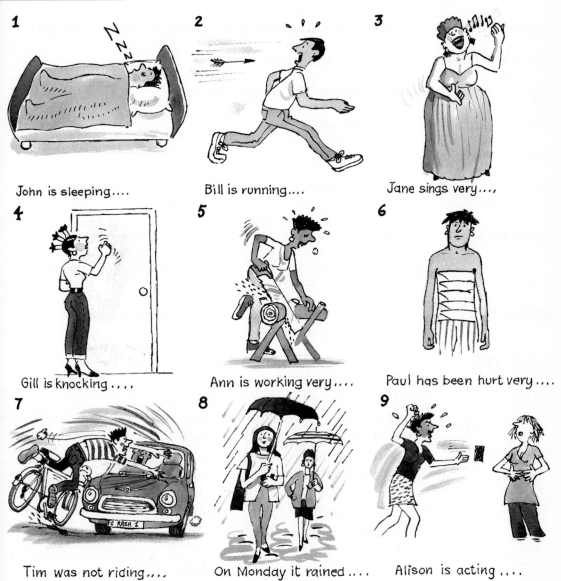

1 John is sleeping....

2 Bill is running....

3 Jane sings very....,

4 Gill is knocking....

5 Ann is working very....

6 Paul has been hurt very....

7 Tim was not riding....,

8 On Monday it rained....

9 Alison is acting....,

KEY

1 John is sleeping soundly/deeply.
2 Bill is running fast/quickly.
3 Jane sings very well/beautifully.
4 Gill is knocking loudly/angrily.
5 Ann is working very hard.
6 Paul has been hurt very badly.
7 Tim was not riding carefully.
8 On Monday it rained heavily.
9 Alison is acting violently.

5.9 Which preposition?

CLASSIFICATION   G.PREP2/1 = Grammar. Prepositions. Complex meaning/1

LANGUAGE FOCUS   Prepositions with verbs

LEVEL   Intermediate to Upper intermediate

AGE   Adolescent/adult

ACTIVITY TYPE   Practice activity

AIM   To give you practice in putting the right preposition with the right verb.

PREPARATION   To do this activity you need to know a lot of set verb/preposition combinations (see A J Thompson & A V Martinet, *A Practical English Grammar*, sections 362–3, or see H Gethin, *Grammar in Context*, pages 186–189).

INSTRUCTIONS   On a separate piece of paper, write out the sentences below and fill in the missing prepositions.

TASK SHEET   1 I must apologize . . . not replying sooner, but I'm afraid I've been rather busy lately.

2 My wife doesn't approve . . . smoking.

3 Do you believe . . . exercising regularly?

4 I look forward . . . seeing you again.

5 Now then, Ben, remember that I'm relying . . . you to see that there's no trouble at the party on Saturday.

6 I get very annoyed . . . people who don't queue at bus stops.

7 The piece of paper burst . . . flames.

8 One person I always laugh . . . when I see him on television is Russ Abbot.

9 I think my girlfriend is getting tired . . . me.

10 Who is responsible . . . spilling milk over the table?

11 My secretary is always complaining . . . her husband.

12 My brother once confided . . . me that he had always wanted to become a skier.

13 It amazes me how some women can cope . . . both a job and a family.

14 There can't be many people in the world who have never heard . . . Margaret Thatcher.

15 I object . . . the way some people don't think you can do the job just because you happen to be a woman.

This exercise is adapted from Peter Watcyn-Jones, *Test Your Own Vocabulary – Book 3* (1985).

1 for   **2** of   **3** in   **4** to   **5** on   **6** with   **7** into   **8** at   **9** of   **10** for
11 about   **12** in   **13** with   **14** of   **15** to.

Comments to the teacher

Phrasal verbs can occur in either the Grammar or Vocabulary sections, depending on which aspect of them is being dealt with.

Vocabulary

Acquiring new vocabulary is an enjoyable experience for most students. For many years in language teaching the tendency was somewhat to neglect vocabulary in order to concentrate on the teaching of structure. Students, however, have always known instinctively how useful and important it is to be able to express meanings through lexis. The recent revival of interest in vocabulary teaching indicates that the language teaching profession has now also come round to this view.

The integral relationship between acquiring new words and improved ability to communicate in the language is reminiscent of the 'chicken and egg' question. It is difficult to say which comes first. It is certainly true that the wider the vocabulary, the easier the tasks of speaking, writing, listening, and reading become. It is also true, however, that the more students hear, read, and use new vocabulary the more they will learn words and remember them.

This section will look at seven different ways of working on and acquiring vocabulary:
1 using a dictionary
2 text-based vocabulary work
3 topic-based vocabulary work
4 word-building (affixes, etc.)
5 idiomatic language (idioms, proverbs, phrasal verbs, etc.)
6 games and puzzles.
7 word associations.

To begin with, however, we look at how to prepare students for self-access vocabulary work.

Different students have different preferred ways of setting about expanding their vocabulary. A study guide such as 5.10 can raise students' awareness of how they learn while providing them with pathways into the Vocabulary section. It is a good idea to prepare a study guide (see 5.11) with advice on how to help themselves remember the new vocabulary.

5.10 Learning new vocabulary

CLASSIFICATION   V.PR/1 = Vocabulary. Preparation/1

LEVEL   Intermediate upwards

AGE   Adolescent/adult

ACTIVITY TYPE   Study guide

AIM   To make you think about how *you* like to learn vocabulary and to show you the kinds of activities which best suit you and your learning style.

PREPARATION   People have different methods of learning new vocabulary. What do *you* do in order to learn new vocabulary?

INSTRUCTIONS   Look at the following statements. Which one(s) do you agree with ?

QUESTIONNAIRE   1 I learn new vocabulary by reading or listening to English. In this way I often 'pick up' new words without having to learn them consciously.

2 I like learning new vocabulary based on a theme or topic. It helps me to remember words if they are connected in this way.

3 I find it helpful to learn the meanings of prefixes and suffixes. It often helps me to guess the meaning of a word that I don't know.

4 I need to learn English idioms and proverbs. And I also need to learn more phrasal verbs.

5 I learn vocabulary best when it is something that I *need* such as when I want to say something but don't have the right word, or I hear or read a word or expression that I don't know. This makes me look up the word I need and learn it for next time.

6 Learning vocabulary can be boring. I like to use word games such as crossword puzzles to increase my vocabulary. In that way I can learn and do something amusing at the same time.

7 I find it easy to learn words which sound interesting, like 'hullabaloo', or which make me think of pleasant things, like 'honey', 'lullaby', or 'skylark'.

COMMENTARY   Look at the commentary or commentaries below which correspond(s) to the number(s) you agreed with.

1 This is a very good way of expanding your vocabulary because you learn new words in context and you can hear or see how they are actually used. You should try some work on the 'Text-based' vocabulary section.

2 This is a useful way of learning vocabulary and it shows that you like to be systematic. You should try some work on the 'Topic-based' vocabulary section.

3 This shows a very thorough approach to learning vocabulary and is especially useful if you need to do a lot of reading in English. You should try some work on the 'Word-building' vocabulary section.

4 Idiomatic language is very important and very useful, especially if you need to speak and listen to English. But be careful that you do not try to learn lists of idioms and phrasal verbs taken out of context and without fully understanding how they are used. You should try some work on the 'Idiomatic language' section.

5 This is a good way to expand vocabulary. A word that you learn because you discover you need it, is often more memorable than words learnt for other reasons. Make sure that you have enough contact with the language to give you plenty of opportunities for expanding your vocabulary in this way. You should try some work on 'Using a dictionary' vocabulary section.

6 Doing word games can be an enjoyable way of learning new vocabulary. Try working on the 'Games and puzzles' vocabulary section. Do remember, though, that most word games use single words out of context, so it might also be a good idea to do some activities from the 'Text-based' section.

7 Words often stick in our mind because they strike us as unusual in some way, or because they remind us of something. A good way to remember the words you learn is to make some link in your mind between the new word and something else. The link may be to something that happened to you when you were a child. Perhaps the link is an unexpected one, something personal. Try working on the 'Word associations' vocabulary section.

Comments to the teacher

The commentary sheet can thus be used to direct students to the sections that best suit them and the way they like to work. The commentary can also point out the advantages and short-comings, if any, of the various methods they use. What is most important is that students should think about how they set about enlarging their vocabulary and that they become aware of other methods which may be more appropriate for certain situations and needs.

5.11 Remember more words!

CLASSIFICATION   V.PR/2 = Vocabulary. Preparation/2

LEVEL   Lower intermediate upwards

AGE   Adolescent/adult

ACTIVITY TYPE   Study guide

AIM   To start you thinking about different ways of remembering the new vocabulary you learn.

PREPARATION   Think about what you do when you learn a new word. Do you have any method for making sure you remember the word and can use it again when you need it? If so, what method(s) do you use?

INSTRUCTIONS   Think about the ways of recording and learning vocabulary described below. Which do you use now? Which new methods would you like to try? Are there any methods you use which are not written down here?

STUDY GUIDE   **1 Vocabulary notebooks**
This is probably the most common method of keeping a record of new words learnt. But there are many different ways of organizing vocabulary notebooks. Which way do you use?

a. Alphabetically: a page or two is set aside for each letter of the alphabet and new words or expressions beginning with that letter are added to the pages.

b. English/English: the new word(s) and the definition are written in English.

c. Translations: the new word(s) is translated into your own language.

d. Pictures: where possible, pictures are drawn to show the meaning of new words.

e. By topic: each topic has a page or two, or more pages and words and expressions connected with the topic are recorded there.

f. By topic network: each topic is recorded by means of a topic network. Each network can be given a whole page.

g. By day: the new words you learn each day can be written on the same page, almost like a diary.

h. Grammatical categories: pages of the vocabulary book are headed: 'Verb', 'Noun', 'Adjective', etc. and each new word is written under the right heading. If the new word has any 'relations', they are written in under the right heading too.

Below are extracts from seven vocabulary notebooks. Each extract corresponds to one of the descriptions above. On a separate piece of paper, write the letter of the written description which corresponds to each extract. (One extract fits two of the descriptions.) One has been done for you as an example.

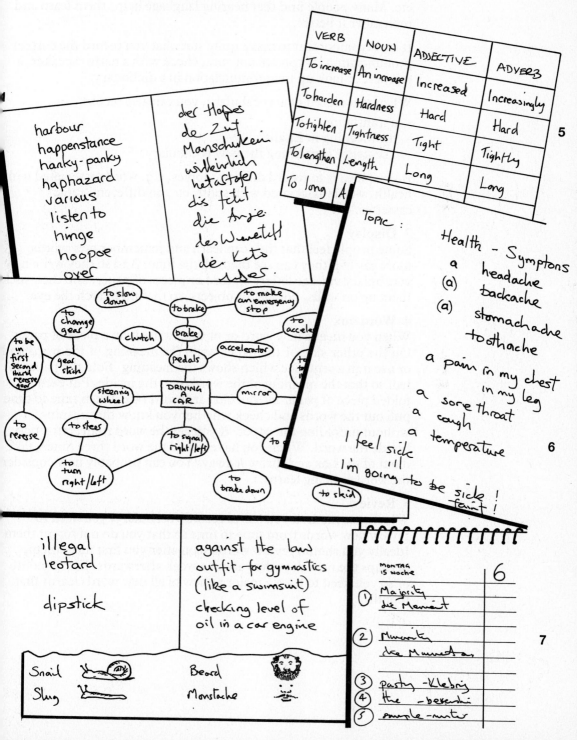

VERB	NOUN	ADJECTIVE	ADVERB	
To increase	An increase	Increased	Increasingly	
To harden	Hardness	Hard		
To tighten	Tightness	Tight	Hard	
To lengthen	Length		Tightly	
To long	A	Long	Long	5
			Long	

harbour
happenstance
hanky-panky
haphazard
various
listen to
hinge
hoopoe
over

der Hafes
de Zut
Manschukein
willkinlich
hetastofen
dis felit
die Angie
des Wenetift
der Keto
relses.

to slow down
to brake
to make an emergency stop
to change gear
clutch
brake
to accele
to be in first second third reverse gear
gear stick
pedals
accelerator
steering wheel
DRIVING A CAR
mirror
to reverse
to steer
to signal right/left
to
to turn right/left
to brake down
to skid

TOPIC :

Health - Symptons
a   headache
(a)   backache
(a)   stomach ache
toothache
a pain in my chest
in my leg
a sore throat
a cough
a temperature   6
I feel sick
I'm going to be sick !
ill   faint !

illegal
leotard

dipstick

against the law
outfit for gymnastics
(like a swimsuit)
checking level of
oil in a car engine

Snail
Slug

Beard
Monstache

MONTAG
15 woche   6
① Majority
die Manait
② Muarity   7
die Munnetas
③ pasty -Klebrig
④ the -berenhi
⑤ example -munter

2 Recording onto cassette

Many English words sound completely different from the way they look when they are written down. For this reason, it is a good idea to record new words and expressions on to a cassette which you can listen to several times while driving, going for a walk, washing up, etc. Many people find that hearing language helps them learn and remember it better.

It is very important to make quite sure that you record the correct pronunciation. If you are not sure, check with a native speaker, a teacher, or look up the pronunciation in a dictionary.

When you record new vocabulary, you can also record:
- a translation
- the meaning in English
- a sentence containing the new vocabulary.

A good idea is to record different topics, e.g. words associated with health, words associated with sport, etc. on different 'topic' cassettes.

3 Display

Some people feel that they can learn and remember new words more easily if they can see them all the time. And so they write new vocabulary in large letters on card or pieces of paper, and then stick them up on walls, boards, or objects, so that they catch the eye.

4 Word box

When you meet a new word or phrase, write it on a piece of paper. On the other side of the paper write the meaning of the word and or use it in a sentence which shows the meaning. Fold the paper in half so that the meaning of the word is on the inside. Put each folded piece of paper into an old cardboard box. From time to time, pull out the words and check whether you know the meaning without unfolding the paper. If you get the word right, put a tick beside the word. When you have ticked the word three times, take it out of the box and throw it away. You can probably now consider the word as being learnt!

5 Review

Whichever method you use to record vocabulary, you need to review new words from time to time so that you do not forget them. Ideally you should review words soon after you first meet them, perhaps the next day, then about a week afterwards. Every month or so you need to have a major review of all new words learnt that month.

1 Using a dictionary

This section does not deal with the study skills involved in using a dictionary (for which see 'Basic study skills' in Chapter 2), but rather contains vocabulary enrichment activities of various types for which students will probably need to use dictionaries.

Synonyms
There are many kinds of vocabulary activities which are based on the finding of synonyms. Such activities are fairly easy to produce and are popular with students (see 5.12).

Homonyms
Dictionary activities are naturally suited to the exploration of words with more than one meaning (see 5.13).

Vocabulary enrichment
One communication strategy used by foreign language students is the strategy of simplification. Simplification of vocabulary is a particularly commonly used strategy in the heat of 'real-time' communication, and such behaviour can be a useful aid to fluency. Nevertheless, during the calm of private study, it can do more advanced students no harm at all to be forced to do the opposite from time to time, i.e. set them activities which demand that simple, over-used words be replaced with richer, more sophisticated vocabulary (see 5.14).

5.12 Similar meanings

CLASSIFICATION	V.UD/1 = Vocabulary. Using a dictionary/1
LEVEL	Upper intermediate to Advanced
AGE	Young adult/adult
ACTIVITY TYPE	Discovery task and practice activity
EQUIPMENT	A good English/English dictionary for students of English.
AIM	To help you widen your vocabulary by looking at words and phrases with similar meanings.
TASK SHEET	1 Find the pairs of words in this list which have similar meanings, for example, *wonderful/marvellous*.

wonderful, halt, ascend, common, stop, immense, commence, beginning, go, marvellous, rise, colossal, exact, vulgar, origin, begin, depart, precise.

2 Pair each of the words in list A below with a phrase of similar meaning in list B, e.g. *verify = prove the truth of*.

A abound, ban, excel, calm, insignificant, acquaint, behave, recall, swell, verify.

B be rich in, make aware of, bring to mind, make an end to, act with propriety, be better than, matter-of-fact, grow larger, of no consequence, prove the truth of.

3 Copy the words in the left-hand box below onto a piece of paper. Then pair a word from the right-hand box with one from the left-hand box, for example, *infirmity = ill health*.

infirmity	moodiness		ill humour	ill-favoured
unlucky	rude		ill-advised	ill-gotten
unwise	churlish		ill health	ill-fated
hostility	stolen		ill-bred	ill-natured
ugly			ill will	

4 Which word is wrongly included in each of these lists of words of similar meaning? Write your answers on a separate piece of paper.

a. tasty, delicious, savoury, interesting, piquant, appetizing, luscious, sweet.

b. nonsensical, absurd, ridiculous, foolish, stupid, irrational, crazy, daft, beastly, unreasonable.

c. morale, spirit, moral, confidence, cheerfulness.

d. murder, kill, die, slaughter, slay, destroy, liquidate.

KEY

1 wonderful/marvellous, halt/stop, ascend/rise, common/vulgar, immense/colossal, commence/begin, beginning/origin, go/depart, exact/precise.

2 abound = be rich in; ban = make an end to; excel = be better than; calm = matter-of-fact; insignificant = of no consequence; acquaint = make aware of; behave = act with propriety; recall = bring to mind; swell = grow larger; verify = prove the truth of.

3 infirmity = ill health   moodiness = ill humour
    unlucky = ill-fated   rude = ill-bred
    unwise = ill-advised   churlish = ill-natured
    hostility = ill will   stolen = ill-gotten
    ugly = ill-favoured

4 a. interesting
   b. beastly
   c. moral
   d. die

Comments to the teacher

Exactly the same sort of activities can be used for antonyms.

5.13 Connections

CLASSIFICATION   V.UD/2 = Vocabulary. Using a dictionary/2

LEVEL   Upper intermediate to Advanced

AGE   Adolescent/adult

ACTIVITY TYPE   Discovery task and practice activity

EQUIPMENT   A good English/English dictionary for students of English.

AIM   To widen your vocabulary by looking at some words with two meanings.

INSTRUCTIONS   1 The words in each of the centre circles below have at least two meanings. For each word in a centre circle find one word from the left-hand column and one word from the right-hand column which are both similar in meaning to that centre word. Be careful, the two words you find will not have the same meaning as each other.
2 The first one has been done for you as an example.

TASK SHEET

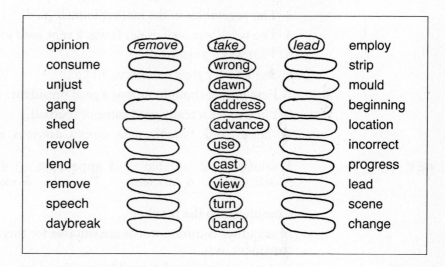

KEY   take – remove, lead; wrong – unjust, incorrect; dawn – daybreak, beginning; address – speech, location; advance – lend, progress; use – consume, employ; cast – shed, mould; view – opinion, scene; turn – revolve, change; band – gang, strip.

Comments to the teacher

For lower level students make an activity on homonyms easier by blanking out the word in two sentences which illustrate the two different meanings.

5.14 Choosing your words

CLASSIFICATION	V.UD/3 = Vocabulary. Using a dictionary/3
LEVEL	Intermediate
AGE	Young adult/adult
ACTIVITY TYPE	Discovery task and practice activity
EQUIPMENT	A good English/English dictionary for students of English.
AIM	To enrich your vocabulary by looking for alternative words for *good*.
INSTRUCTIONS	Copy these sentences onto a sheet of paper, replacing the word *good* with a more precise word from the list below. None of the words should be used more than once. Make use of your dictionary where necessary.

TASK SHEET

1 St Francis of Assisi was a *good* man.
2 These tools are not *good* for the job we have to do.
3 The vegetables in the market looked *good*.
4 The work was well done. It was a very *good* job.
5 That was a *good* meal.
6 She's a very *good* secretary.
7 Few people thought he was a *good* president.
8 I like to see a really *good* game of football.

skilful, exciting, suitable, wise, saintly, delicious, efficient, appetizing.

KEY

1 saintly	2 suitable	3 appetizing	4 skilful
5 delicious	6 efficient	7 wise	8 exciting.

Comments to the teacher

Many other common words are suitable for this kind of treatment, e.g.

bad, nice, lovely, awful, terrible, get, thing, etc.

2 Text-based vocabulary work

It is a well-established technique to use a text as a basis for vocabulary work. The great advantage of text-based vocabulary work is that unfamiliar lexis is contextualized. This means that students have a better chance of acquiring the full and correct meaning in that context, and also a better chance of remembering the words. A number of different techniques and activity types for exploiting texts for vocabulary work are included below. (The texts used are all written texts for the sake of convenience, but these techniques for vocabulary enrichment can be used equally well with spoken texts, recorded on cassette.)

Related words
A text can be used as a springboard in that some of the words in it can be explored in a way which goes beyond their use in that particular context. Many students, for example, when they encounter a new word, like to learn all grammatically-related forms of the new word at the same time. That is to say, that if they encounter a word like *aggravate* in its verbal form, they would like also to know that the noun *aggravation* exists, and also that there is a difference in stress pattern between the two words. In this way, students get several new words for the price of one, so to speak. Another way of expanding on vocabulary in the text is to look at words which stand in some kind of *lexical* relation to the words chosen, such as synonyms, antonyms, superordinates, etc (see 5.15).

Guessing meaning from the context
Teaching students the skill of guessing the meaning of unknown words in context is probably the most useful kind of text-based vocabulary work in terms of long-term gain. It is a skill which fluent readers and listeners employ frequently and the ability to deduce meaning in this way, or at least to limit the possibilities of meaning effectively, correlates highly with all-round language performance.

In addition to *practice* in guessing words from context, there is also a need for learner training in how to approach a text containing unknown words (see 5.16).

5.15 The waiter

CLASSIFICATION	V.TB/1 = Vocabulary. Text-based work/1
LEVEL	Upper intermediate to Advanced
AGE	Adult
ACTIVITY TYPE	Discovery task and practice activity
AIM	To widen your vocabulary by reading a text and looking at words related to some of the vocabulary in the text.
PREPARATION	Read the text below. If there are any words you do not understand, try to guess the meaning. If necessary, look them up in a dictionary.

INSTRUCTIONS   Read the text carefully, then do the tasks which follow.

TASK SHEET   'They sat at a table near the window, and were waited on by a tall, fat, pale Frenchman with a Bourbon nose who was pompous and superior to the verge of bursting. His fat white face and his little scornful eyes irritated Julia. She thought that she would like to turn round and say something rude to him. Just one word – one little word – to see the expression on his face when she said it.

Then food and the rosy lights comforted her. She began to feel aloof and she forgot the waiter.'

From *After Leaving Mr Mackenzie* by Jean Rhys.

1 Copy and fill in the table below with the parts of speech related to the words from the text which have already been inserted. If you think a relevant part of speech does not exist, draw a line (–). Underline the stressed syllable of words with more than one syllable. The first one has been done for you.

Adjective	Verb	Noun
pale pompous superior scornful	to pale irritate	paleness/palour verge

2 Copy and fill in the table below giving a word with a similar meaning and a word opposite in meaning to each of the adjectives listed from the text. Find similar and opposite meanings to the adjectives as they are used in this text. Choose your answers from the words in italics below the table. Use a dictionary to help you. Some of them have already been done for you.

Adjective	Similar meaning	Opposite meaning
rude pompous pale scornful superior aloof	shocking haughty	 modest involved

disdainful, involved, pasty, distant, humble, shocking, respectful, placatory, self-important, ruddy, haughty, modest.

KEY

Adjective	Verb	Noun
pale	pale	palour
pompous	—	pomposity
superior	—	superiority
scornful	scorn	scorn
irritating	irritate	irritation
verging (on)	verge (on)	verge

Adjective	Similar meaning	Opposite meaning
rude	shocking	placatory
pompous	self-important	modest
pale	pasty	ruddy
scornful	disdainful	respectful
superior	haughty	humble
aloof	distant	involved

5.16 New words in difficult texts

CLASSIFICATION   V.TB/2 = Vocabulary. Text-based work/2

LEVEL   Intermediate to Advanced

AGE   Adolescent/adult

ACTIVITY TYPE   Study guide

AIM   To help you cope with new, unknown words when you are reading.

STUDY GUIDE   1 If you keep stopping to look up words in the dictionary while you are reading, your progress may be slow and you may forget many of the words. This is because you are trying to do two things at once: reading and understanding at the same time as looking up and learning new words.

2 Here is a suggested approach to a more difficult text:

   a. Never look up a word until you have read the whole context. Therefore, always read at least to the end of the sentence, perhaps to the end of the paragraph.

   b. Try to guess the meaning from the context, before turning to the dictionary.

   c. For each text (or book) that you read, make a special vocabulary list of words that are often used. This will save you looking in the dictionary each time. Remember to learn the pronunciation at this stage. Even when you are reading silently, you may 'think' the correct pronunciation.

3 If you are going to read the text again, keep the special vocabulary list with it. Otherwise, add the words to your main vocabulary list.

(From *Use Your Dictionary* by Adrian Underhill.)

3 Topic-based vocabulary work

Learning vocabulary which is associated with a particular topic is a very popular method of vocabulary extension with students who feel that there is something systematic about such a method. In addition, the immediate usefulness of what they have learnt is more apparent than when they just learn lists of unrelated words. Their instincts in this respect may well be more reliable than they know. Many researchers in cognitive science now believe that we store words in our brains in meaning networks and that activating one 'node' of a meaning network alerts other parts of the network to be ready. If words are stored in this way in the brain, then they may well be easier to remember if they are learnt in this way.

The topic may be presented via a text or using a picture or pictures, as in these examples.

5.17 The senses

CLASSIFICATION	V.TO/1 = Vocabulary. Topic/1
LEVEL	Lower intermediate to Intermediate
AGE	Adolescent/adult
TOPIC	Personal – the senses
ACTIVITY TYPE	Discovery task and practice activity
AIM	To practise and learn new vocabulary for how things taste, smell, and feel.
PREPARATION	People have five senses: sight, hearing, taste, smell, and touch. Do you know enough English words to describe things in this way?
INSTRUCTIONS	Copy and fill in the gaps in the sentences below with the word for the noun shown in the picture, and one or two appropriate adjectives chosen from the list in italics. The first sentence has been done for you.
TASK SHEET	*slippery, soft, heavy, cold, light, furry, hard, prickly, bitter, rough, scented, sharp, wet, slimy, hot, smooth, sweet.*

1 Ice feels smooth and cold.

2 A ..... feels..... and.....

3 A ...... smells......

4 ..... tastes .....

5 The ..... feels .....

6 A...... tastes .....

7 An ..... feels ..... and .....

8 .... feels ..... and .....

9 ....., tastes ....., and ......

10 A ..... feels ..... and.....

11 A ....., feels ..... and.....

12 A ..... feels ....., and .....

13 ..... feels .....

14 A ...... feels .....

15 A....., feels .....

KEY

Ice feels smooth and cold.

A feather feels light and soft.

A flower/rose smells scented.

Chocolate tastes sweet.

The sun feels hot.

6 A lemon tastes bitter.

7 An axe feels hard and sharp.

8 Soap feels smooth and slippery.

9 Ice cream tastes cold and sweet.

10 A cat feels soft and furry.

11 A coconut feels hard and rough.

12 A cactus feels sharp and prickly.

13 Rain feels wet.

14 A fish feels smooth/wet/slimy/slippery.

15 A weight feels heavy.

Comments to the teacher
The pictures in this exercise would also work very well for an exercise on articles; instead of the nouns and adjectives, the articles could be blanked out.

4 Word building

'Word building' is the term generally used of this area of vocabulary work but, in fact, it is much more a question of 'word dismantlement', seeing how a word is made up and using this discovery to help interpret its meaning and grammatical function in a sentence. A study of the meaning of common word roots and affixes is a vital tool in this process.

5.18 Making things happen

CLASSIFICATION   V.WB/1 = Vocabulary. Word building/1

LEVEL   Intermediate

AGE   Young adult

ACTIVITY TYPE   Study guide and practice activities

AIM   To help you use and recognize verbs ending in -en, -ify, -ize.

PREPARATION   1 In order to understand this study guide and do the activities, you need to understand the meaning of the words: *suffix* and *syllable*. If you are not sure what these words mean, do activity W.SP/1 first and then come back to this activity.

2 In English, verbs can be made by adding certain endings on to adjectives and nouns. This study guide will look at verbs made in the following ways:
– add -en to one syllable adjectives, e.g. *hard + en = harden*
– add -ify to one syllable nouns and adjectives, e.g. *class + ify = classify*
– add -ize to nouns and adjectives with two or more syllables, e.g. *legal + ize = legalize*.

INSTRUCTIONS   Read the information below and do the practice activities.

TASK SHEET   **1 The suffix -en**
This suffix forms verbs from adjectives of one syllable. It may mean 'become' or sometimes 'grow'. Copy out and complete these sentences. The first one has been done for you as an example.

1 The sky became bright. *The sky brightened*.
2 The sky grew red. The sky . . .
3 The sky grew dark. The sky . . .
4 The glue became hard. The glue . . .
5 The sea became rough. The sea . . .
6 The fruit became ripe. The fruit . . .
7 The tar became soft. The tar . . .
8 The rope became tight. The rope . . .
9 The wind grew fresh. The wind . . .
10 His attitude became tough. His attitude . . .

2 The suffix *-ify*

This suffix is added to both nouns and adjectives (of Latin origin)
if they have one syllable. Copy out and complete the sentences
below. The first one has been done for you as an example.

1 He made the water pure. *He purified the water*.
2 He made the system simple. He . . . the system.
3 They made their evidence false. They . . . their evidence.
4 He formed the laws into a code. He c . . . the laws.
5 He arranged the material in classes. He c . . . the material.

3 The suffix *-ize*

This suffix is added to nouns and adjectives (mainly of Latin and
Greek origin), if they have two or more syllables. (**Note:** the
spelling *-ise* is also possible.) Copy out and complete the sentences
below. The first one has been done for you as an example.

1		
	made	
	turned	
He	changed	the liquid into atoms.
	converted	
	transformed	

He atomized the liquid.
2 He turned the fruit into liquid. He l . . . the fruit.
3 She made the man into her idol. She i . . . the man.
4 They made a summary of the report. They s . . . the report.
5 They turned the island into a colony. They c . . . the island.
6 They stated the information item by item. They i . . . the
information.

Adapted from *Using English Suffixes and Prefixes* by Tom
McArthur (1972).

2 The sky reddened; 5 The sea roughened; 8 The rope tightened;
3 The sky darkened; 6 The fruit ripened; 9 The wind freshened;
4 The glue hardened; 7 The tar softened; .10 His attitude toughened

2 He simplified the system; 4 He codified the laws;
3 They falsified their evidence; 5 He classified the material.

2 He liquidized the fruit; 5 They colonized the island;
3 She idolized the man; 6 They itemized the information.
4 They summarized the report;

5 Idiomatic language

5.19 Beastly idioms

CLASSIFICATION	**V.ID/1 = Vocabulary. Idiomatic language/1**
LEVEL	**Lower intermediate to Advanced**
AGE	**Adolescent/adult**
ACTIVITY TYPE	**Discovery task and practice activity**
AIM	To learn and practise idioms containing references to animals.
EQUIPMENT	A dictionary of idioms or a good English/English dictionary which contains idioms.
INSTRUCTIONS	Copy out the sentences below and complete them by choosing the correct idiom. The first one has been done for you as an example.
TASK SHEET	Michelle has this annoying habit of interrupting you in the middle of a sentence. She never lets you finish what you want to say. . . *cook one's goose/get one's goat/make a beast of oneself* *It really gets my goat.*

1 I'd rather visit George tomorrow on the way back from Peter's. We could then . . . as it would save us having to make two separate journeys.
kill two birds with one stone/hold one's horses/flog a dead horse

2 Oh dear – I'm beginning to get nervous now. I always . . . just before an exam starts, don't you?
have butterflies in one's stomach/go at snail's pace/smell a rat

3 How do you know that Ed is going to be posted to Madrid? Nobody else seems to know anything about it. – Oh, I . . . , Ed's boss.
be top dog/take the bull by the horns/get it from the horse's mouth

4 Tim Spence didn't stop eating yesterday at the party. I've never seen a child of his age eat so much! He had cakes and biscuits in both hands all the time. He really . . .
be a fly in the ointment/make a pig of oneself/go at a snail's pace

5 Jim is really enjoying living out in the country. He says he . . . every day for a run before breakfast, and he's never felt better.
have other fish to fry/get up with the lark/let sleeping dogs lie

From *Idioms in Practice* by Jennifer Seidl.

1 kill two birds with one stone (achieve two objectives by doing one thing)

2 have butterflies in my stomach (feel extremely nervous, often before a performance of some kind)

3 got it from the horse's mouth (get information direct from the source – this idiom came from betting on horse races)

4 made a pig of himself (was extremely greedy)

5 gets up with the lark (gets up very early – a lark is a kind of bird)

5.20 Work it out!

CLASSIFICATION   **V.ID/2 = Vocabulary. Idiomatic language/2**

LEVEL   **Lower intermediate to Intermediate**

AGE   **Adolescent/young adult**

ACTIVITY TYPE   **Practice activity**

AIM   To practise some common phrasal verbs.

INSTRUCTIONS   Complete the phrasal verbs with one of the prepositions given.

TASK SHEET   *off, after, to, for, down, out, on, back, away, in, up, over.*

1 take off   2 look...   3 ring...   4 take...

5 run...   6 listen...   7 knock...   8 clear...

9 cut...   10 fill...   11 look...   12 try...

1 take off	**4** take back	**7** knock out	**10** fill in
2 look after	**5** run over	**8** clear away	**11** look for
3 ring up	**6** listen to	**9** cut down	**12** try on

5.21 Folk wisdom

CLASSIFICATION	**V.ID/3 = Vocabulary. Idiomatic language/3**
LEVEL	**Intermediate to Advanced**
AGE	**Young adult/adult**
ACTIVITY TYPE	**Discovery task and reflection**
AIM	To learn or revise proverbs and to reflect on whether they are true or not.
PREPARATION	Many proverbs reflect folk wisdom, generally held views about everyday life which are passed on from generation to generation in this way. When people quote these proverbs, they often make it clear that they are doing just that by adding phrases like: '. . . as the saying goes', 'You know what they say . . .' etc. Very often too, people do not quote the whole proverb but just enough for people to recognize it, e.g. 'too many cooks spoil the broth', may be quoted as simply 'too many cooks . . .'
INSTRUCTIONS	Read the dialogues below. Each dialogue contains a proverb (in *italics*) which expresses a bit of folk wisdom. For each dialogue: – explain the meaning of each proverb in your own words – say whether an equivalent proverb exists in your own language – say whether you agree with the sentiment expressed.
TASK SHEET	1 Janet didn't seem to care very much about Paul before he went away, but now she writes to him every day.' 'Ah well, *absence makes the heart grow fonder*, so they say.'
	2 'My uncle's coming to visit me next week.' 'I didn't know you had an uncle.' 'Well, we hardly ever see him. He's a sales executive with a big multi-national company. He's lived and worked in every continent, and he travels almost continuously.' 'Has he got any family?' 'Never had the time. How does the saying go? *A rolling stone gathers no moss.*'
	3 'I feel exhausted. I hardly got any sleep last night at all. There was a loud teenage party going on next door. I think it went on all night.' 'Didn't the parents put a stop to it?' 'Well, they're away for a few days. I guess it's a case of *while the cat's away . . . (the mice will play).*'
	4 'Bill is so helpful. He's been offering to help paint the church hall for weeks now, but he's very busy of course, so I don't think he's done it yet.'

'Well, Charlie painted the whole hall last Saturday without saying a word to anyone. *Actions speak louder than words*, so they say.'
'Well, I never!'

5 'Sometimes I wonder when we're ever going to get this job finished. We seem to have been at it for ages!'
'Oh, come on! *Rome wasn't built in a day*, you know.'

6 'Sorry I'm late. I tried to take a short-cut but I wasn't absolutely sure about it and in the end I got completely lost and ended up miles away over the other side of town.'
'Sounds like a case of *more haste, less speed*.'

COMMENTARY

1 When people go away, we appreciate them more than when they are with us.

2 People who travel a lot or who move very often do not make a lot of friends and/or do not get married or have loved ones about them.

3 When a person or people in a position of authority are away, those who are normally subject to that authority will take advantage of their absence to behave in a way which would not be allowed if they were present.

4 It is better to actually do something than talk about doing it. Also, people who talk about what they are going to do, do not always fulfill their promises.

5 A big or important job/project can not be rushed and will inevitably take a long time.

6 If you try to do things too quickly, you will make mistakes and, in the end, it will take longer to do than if you had taken your time and proceeded carefully.

6 Games and puzzles

Word games and puzzles are attractive and motivating – people do them in their own language for relaxation and entertainment. At the same time, they can be very instructive and can help foreign students increase their vocabulary in a relatively painless way.

There is a great variety of word games. This section gives just three examples of puzzle types which are easy for teachers to construct, but there are many more possibilities to explore.

5.22 Thematic crossword

CLASSIFICATION	**V.GP/1 = Vocabulary. Games and puzzles/1**
LEVEL	**Intermediate**
AGE	**Adolescent/adult**
TOPIC	**Places**
ACTIVITY TYPE	**Thematic crossword**
AIM	To practise the words for some common places, and to have fun!
PREPARATION	Revise 'places' in your vocabulary notebook.
INSTRUCTIONS	All the clues refer to words for places. Read the clues and fill in 'the name of the place'.

TASK SHEET

1   The place where legal matters are decided.

2   The place where plays and musicals are performed.

3   The place where a town's water supply is stored.

4   The place where young flowers and plants are cultivated.

5   The place in a bank where money and valuables are kept.

6   The place where fish are kept.

7   The place, often in the open, where many different sorts of goods can be bought.

8   The place where wild animals are kept for the public to see.

9   The place where you find other animals such as cows, sheep, chickens, pigs, etc.

10   The place where gas is stored.

11   The place where fruit trees grow.

12   The place in a factory where goods are stored.

13   The place where criminals are kept.

14   The place where they clean clothes, sheets, etc.

15   The place where birds are kept.

16   The place where dead people are buried.

17   The room where doctors receive their patients.

Acknowledgement
Adapted from *Test Your Own Vocabulary* by Peter Watcyn-Jones.

KEY

1 court	**7** market	**13** prison
2 theatre	**8** zoo	**14** laundry
3 reservoir	**9** farm	**15** aviary
4 nursery	**10** laboratory	**16** cemetary
5 vault	**11** orchard	**17** surgery
6 aquarium	**12** warehouse	

Comments to the teacher

This kind of crossword is particularly suitable for pedagogic purposes because:

- it is extremely easy for teachers to construct, whereas a normal crossword is difficult and time-consuming to make
- the thematic aspect is good for vocabulary learning.

5.23 Step by step

CLASSIFICATION   **V.GP/2 = Vocabulary. Games and puzzles/2**

LEVEL   **Lower intermediate**

AGE   **Junior/adolescent**

ACTIVITY TYPE   **Word puzzle**

AIM   To practise vocabulary, and have fun!

PREPARATION   Look at this example of a 'step-by-step' puzzle.
In this example *boy* changes into *man*.
Only one letter changes on each line:

BOY
BAY
MAY
MAN

INSTRUCTIONS   Now you change *sea* into *sky*, and then *land* into *seas*. The sentences at the side will help you find the right word. Write your answers on a separate piece of paper.

TASK SHEET   Morning is the time for the sun to rise. Evening is the time for it to . . .

The policeman got into the car and . . . next to the driver.

What did you . . . ? I can't hear you very well.

SEA
SKY

I've forgotten to bring any money. Can
you . . . me some?

Some people . . . their friends a card
at the New Year.

Good corn grows from good . . .

When someone looks into water he often
. . . his face.

LAND
SEAS

Acknowledgement
Adapted from *Puzzles for English Practice 2* by David Cobb.

KEY

SEA	LAND
SET	LEND
SAT	SEND
SAY	SEED
SKY	SEES
	SEAS

Comments to the teacher

1 This type of puzzle, without the 'helpful' sentences, is popular
with native-speaker children. The addition of the sentences gives
this puzzle a pedagogical dimension and prevents students putting
in words they do not understand.

2 As a variation ask the students to write the 'helpful' sentences.

5.24 Wordsearch

CLASSIFICATION　　V.GP/3 = **Vocabulary. Games and puzzles/3**

LEVEL　　**Advanced**

AGE　　**Adolescent/adult**

TOPIC　　**Everyday life** – food and drink

ACTIVITY TYPE　　**Puzzle**

AIM　　To recognize words connected with eating, and to have fun!

INSTRUCTIONS　　1 Hidden in the square below are ten verbs connected with eating.
The verbs may be written:

a. from left to right → 　　**c.** from top to bottom ↓

b. from right to left ← 　　**d.** from bottom to top ↑

2 Copy the square onto a piece of paper. Then circle the ten verbs.
The first one has been done for you.

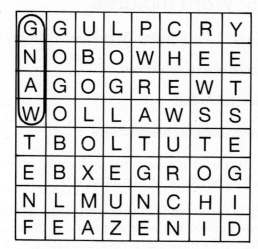

Comments to the teacher

This kind of puzzle can be made much easier by simplifying the vocabulary and also by limiting word arrangement to words that go horizontally and vertically, but not diagonally or from the bottom to top.

7 Word associations

The affective element in acquiring new vocabulary is a very powerful factor and we can encourage students to make use of this dimension in self-access work. This is another area where it is not possible or even appropriate to provide 'correct' answers for the activities, so students need to be aware enough to accept that fact. It is the process which is important here, rather than the end product.

5.25 Word pictures

CLASSIFICATION   V.WA/1 = Vocabulary. Word associations/1

LEVEL   Intermediate to Advanced

AGE   Adolescent/adult

ACTIVITY TYPE   Creative, forming associations

AIM   To help you learn new words by forming links in your mind with something memorable like a picture.

PREPARATION   Think of three words in your own language which you really like. Why do you like them? Is it the sound, the shape, or do they make you think of something pleasant or funny?

INSTRUCTIONS   1 Look up the words you do not know in the list below.

2 Choose six of the words you like best, perhaps because of the sound, perhaps because of the meaning.

3 Draw a picture to illustrate each word. The picture does not have to illustrate the meaning. Use your imagination. The stranger, the better.

4 Write a story connecting the six words you have chosen. Make it as strange or amusing as you like. Then draw a picture to illustrate part of the story.

TASK SHEET

hullabaloo	uproar	shimmering	crotchety
surreptitiously	troglodyte	blossom	vermin
ivory	variegated	titivate	slurp
lullaby	splash	yoyo	sidle

Close your eyes. Think of the words you chose and see in your mind's eye the pictures you drew or go through the story you wrote.

Comments to the teacher

This activity should help students to remember new words because they have been actively involved in forming associations, and the words have some personal significance for them because of the pictures they drew or the story they wrote. For more ideas for affective activities for classroom vocabulary see J Morgan and M Rinvolucri, *Vocabulary* in this series.

Social language

It can be useful in a self-access system to have a section which deals with stock phrases which are the currency of everyday social interaction. The phrases can be organized under various headings: common functions of language such as 'requesting politely', 'apologizing', 'leave-taking', etc; situations or settings such as 'at the hairdressers', 'buying clothes', etc; set responses, including responses to routine actions, such as 'bless you' when someone sneezes.

Ideally, the Keys to this section would be available on cassette as well as in written form. This enables students to pay attention to the pronunciation of these phrases and this is essential if they are to be learnt for use, rather than just as an academic exercise.

5.26 Right answers

CLASSIFICATION	SL.SR/1 = Social language. Set responses/1
LEVEL	**Intermediate to Upper intermediate**
AGE	**Young adult/adult**
ACTIVITY TYPE	**Discovery task and practice activity**
AIM	To learn and practise set phrases and responses in particular situations.
PREPARATION	Look at the pictures below and think about what the people might be saying to one another.
INSTRUCTIONS	Fill in the missing words in the pictures. Choose a phrase from 1–6 and then match a response from phrases a.–f. to fit each picture over the page. Be careful, both lists are in jumbled order.

1 I didn't know John was married.

2 I'm sorry I'm late.

3 Thanks for the flowers, Jim.

4 My father's much better now.

5 Pass the salt, please.

6 You couldn't give me a hand, could you?

a. It's a pleasure.

b. Yes, of course.

c. Oh, that's all right.

d. Certainly. Here you are.

e. Oh, I'm so pleased to hear it.

f. No, neither did I.

KEY   **1** 4e.   **2** 1f.   **3** 5d.   **4** 2c.   **5** 6b.   **6** 3a.

Conclusion

Where do we go from here?

Learner autonomy has been a live issue in English Language
Teaching since the 1960s. In spite of this we find that language
classes and language schools have increased their number rather
than decreased. Students persist in wanting to learn from good
teachers. Does this mean that self-directed learning and learner
independence are unattainable goals? And what is the role of self-
access in all this?

The provision of self-access learning materials can be seen as one
weapon in the wider struggle towards learner independence. Self-
access materials facilitate self-directed learning but they do not
guarantee it (see p. 24). Moreover, it is quite possible to foster an
independent approach to learning without self-access materials.

There are many different ways of focusing on the learner: the needs of the individual can be highlighted — in which case, self-access materials are very useful — and/or the group can be the focus of attention. Approaches which foster group self-direction (rather than individual self-direction) tend not to be so concerned with self-access materials but aim rather to promote group cohesion and shift authority and responsibility from the teacher to the learners as a group. Examples of such approaches include the promotion of group projects and experiential learning (see p. 53), and also the introduction of negotiated syllabuses (where the teacher presides over the negotiation of various aspects of the syllabus and methodology with, and between, learners).

The danger with an approach to learning which is exclusively concerned with the needs of the individual is that it will tend to be very instrumental. Increased knowledge and enhanced skills may result without personal growth towards real independence, or the development of social skills and self-knowledge. On the other hand, an approach which depends entirely on negotiated group decisions sometimes leads to the dominance of some students over others and there is a danger that individual needs are lost sight of in the search for the common good. And what about the role of the teacher? Is it permissable in a learner-centred approach for the teacher to intervene and advise in favour or against a certain course of action? Or is this unwarranted manipulation which will cause learners to continue being dependent on the teacher?

In my view, learner independence is best achieved by combining respect for learners as individuals with respect for learners as members of the group. I also believe that learners – both as individuals and as members of a group – can benefit from the knowledge and skills that teachers bring without necessarily losing their independence. What this seems to suggest is that the ideal learning environment is a combination of:

1 expert help and direction by the teacher where appropriate (this will probably include some quite traditional teacher-directed lessons)

2 group-directed learning (group projects, negotiated syllabuses, etc.)

3 self-access facilities which students can use to work on their individual problems.

These are three different kinds of learning experiences which all enhance learning in a different way. It is to be hoped that the future holds a place for all three approaches.

Appendix 1

Extract from a topic classification system

Main headings

Agriculture	Law
American studies	Leisure activities
The arts	Mass media
British life and	Medicine
institutions	Moral/Social issues
Business/Commerce/	Natural world
Economics	Objects/Implements
Customs/Folklore	People
Developing world	Personal
Education	Places
Employment/Work	Politics
Energy	Relationships
Engineering	Science
Environment	Sociology
Everyday life	Space
Geography	Supernatural
History	Technology/
Industry	Computers
Language and	Transport
communication	Travel

Appendix 2

Text type classification system

Abbreviations	Maps (small format)
Advertisements	Notes/Messages
Anecdotes/Jokes	Newspapers
Articles/Journals	Pictures/Visual
Bibliographies	stimulus
Broadcasts/News	Posters/Notices
Conversations/	Questionnaires
Dialogues	Reports (not student
Discussions/Debates	or course report)
Examination model	Service encounters
answers	Songs
Forms/Applications/	Stories/Narratives
CVs	Tapescripts
Glossaries/Word lists	Telephone
Instructions	conversations
Interviews	Tests/Examinations
Lectures/Talks	Visual information
Letters	(graphs, etc.)

Acknowledgement
The topic and text type classification systems were devised by teachers at the Bell School, Cambridge.

Bibliography

Background reading

Allan D. 1985. *Oxford Placement Tests.* Oxford: Oxford University Press.

Altman H. B. (ed.) 1972. *Individualizing the Foreign Language Classroom.* New York: Newbury House.

Altman H. B. and **James C. V.** (eds.) 1980. *Foreign Language Teaching: Meeting Individual Needs.* Oxford: Pergamon Press.

Carter G. and **Thomas H.** 1986. 'Dear Brown Eyes – experiential learning in a project-oriented approach', *English Language Teaching Journal* Vol. 40/3.

Dickinson L. 'Autonomy, Self-directed Learning and Individualization' in E. Smyth (ed.).

Dickinson L. 1987. *Self-Instruction in Language Learning.* Cambridge: Cambridge University Press.

Diller K. C. (ed.) 1981. *Individual Differences and Universals in Language Learning Aptitude.* New York: Newbury House.

Disick R. S. 1975. *Individualizing Language Instruction.* New York: Harcourt Brace Jovanovich, Inc.

Ellis G. and **Sinclair B.** 1989. *Learning to Learn English.* Cambridge: Cambridge University Press.

Gardner R. C. and **Lambert W. E.** *Attitudes and Motivation in Second Language Learning.* New York: Newbury House.

Geddes M. and **Sturtridge G.** (eds.) 1982.

Individualization. Oxford: Modern English Publications.

Henner-Stanchina C. and **Riley P.** 'Aspects of Autonomous Learning' in E. Smyth (ed).

Naiman N., Fröhlich M., Stern H. H. and **Todesco A.** 1978. *The Good Language Learner.* Research in Education Series, no. 7. Ontario Institute for Studies in Education.

Oskarsson M. 1980. *Approaches to Self-Assessment in Foreign Language Learning.* Oxford: Pergamon Press.

Rodgers T. 1978. 'Strategies for individualized language learning and teaching' in J. C. Richards (ed.) *Understanding Second and Foreign Language Learning: Issues and Approaches.* New York: Newbury House.

Rogers C. R. 1969. *Freedom to Learn.* Columbus, OH: Charles E. Merrill Publishing Co.

Smyth E. (ed.) 1978. *Individualization in Language Learning,* ELT Document 103. London: British Council: ETIC.

Stevick E. W. 1976. *Memory, Meaning & Method.* New York: Newbury House.

Stevick E. W. 1981. *Teaching Languages: A Way and Ways.* New York: Newbury House.

Strevens P. 'The Paradox of Individualized Instruction: It Takes Better Teachers to Focus on the Learner' in Altman H. B. and James C. V. (eds.).

Swan M. and Smith B. 1987. *Learner English*. Cambridge: Cambridge University Press.

Technology

Cooper R., Lavery M., and Rinvolucri M. (forthcoming) *Resource Books for Teachers: Video*. Oxford: Oxford University Press.

Hardisty D. and Windeatt S. (forthcoming) *Resource Books for Teachers: CALL*. Oxford: Oxford University Press.

Jones C. and Fortescue S. 1987. *Computers in the Language Classroom*. London: Longman.

Examinations

General

Davies S. and West R. 1988. *Longman Guide to ELT Examinations*. London: Longman.

O'Dell F. 1987. *English as a Foreign Language: Preliminary Examinations*. London: Longman.

O'Dell F. 1986. *English as a Foreign Language: Intermediate Examinations*. London: Longman.

Cambridge First Certificate

Nolasco R. 1987. *Success at First Certificate – The Interview*. Oxford: Oxford University Press.

Nixon, S. 1987. *Successful Listening for First Certificate*. Oxford: Oxford University Press.

London Chamber of Commerce and Industry

Davies S. *et al.* 1988. *Bilingual Handbooks of Business Correspondence and Communication*. New York: Prentice Hall.

TOEFL

King C. and Stanley N. 1983. *Building Skills for the TOEFL*. Nashville, TN: Nelson.

Mason, V. W. 1989. *Practice Tests for the TOEFL*. (rev. ed.) Nashville, TN: Nelson.

Oxford and ARELS

Richardson V. *et al.* 1988. *Oxford and ARELS Examinations Handbook*. London: Bell & Hyman.

English for Academic Purposes

Adkins A. and McKean I. 1983. *Text to Note*. London: Edward Arnold.

Fletcher M. and Hargreaves R. 1985. *Defining and Verbalising*, in the series Functional Units. London: Bell & Hyman.

Hamp-Lyons L. and Berry Courter K. 1987. *Study Writing*. Cambridge: Cambridge University Press.

Hamp-Lyons L. and Berry Courter K. 1985. *Research Matters*. New York: Prentice Hall.

Heaton J. B. 1975. *Studying in English*. London: Longman.

Johnson K. 1981. *Communicate in Writing*. London: Longman.

Lynch A. 1983. *Study Listening*. Cambridge: Cambridge University Press.

Wallace M. 1980. *Study Skills in English*. Cambridge: Cambridge University Press.

Whitney N. 1984. *Study Skills for Reading*. London: Heinemann.

British / American Life

Brookes H. F. and Fraenkel C. E. 1982. *Life in Britain*. London: Heinemann.

Church N. and Moss A. 1983. *How to Survive in the USA*. Cambridge: Cambridge University Press.

Laird E. 1986. *Faces of Britain*. London: Longman.

Laird E. 1988. *Faces of the USA*. London: Longman.

Munro Mackenzie M. D. and Westward J. 1983. *Background to Britain*. Basingstoke: Macmillan.

Musman R. 1982. *Background to the USA*. London: Longman.

Musman R. 1973. *Britain Today*. London: Longman.

Room A. 1986. *Dictionary of Britain*. Oxford: Oxford University Press.

Sheerin S., Seath J. and White G. 1985. *Spotlight on Britain*. Oxford: Oxford University Press.

Project Work

Fried-Booth D. L. 1986. *Resource Books for Teachers: Project Work*. Oxford: Oxford University Press.

Reading

Grellet F. 1981. *Developing Reading Skills*. Cambridge: Cambridge University Press.

Greenwood J. 1988. *Resource Books for Teachers: Class Readers*. Oxford: Oxford University Press.

Jolly D. 1982. *Reading Choices*. Cambridge: Cambridge University Press.

Nuttall C. 1982. *Teaching Reading Skills in a Foreign Language*. London: Heinemann.

Williams E. 1984. *Reading in the Language Classroom*. Basingstoke: Macmillan.

Listening

(See under **Pronunciation** for material with contextualized minimal pairs.)

General

Davies P. and Rinvolucri M. 1988. *Cambridge Handbooks for Language Teachers: Dictation*. Cambridge: Cambridge University Press.

For information transfer exercises

Blundell L. and Stokes J. 1981. *Task Listening*. Cambridge: Cambridge University Press.

Ur P. 1984. *Teaching Listening Comprehension*. Cambridge: Cambridge University Press.

For children

Scott W. 1980. *Are You Listening?*. Oxford: Oxford University Press.

For interpretive listening

Maley A. and Duff A. 1978. *Variations on a Theme*. Cambridge: Cambridge University Press

For authentic material for extended listening

Cobb D. and Dalley J. 1980–87. *Sherlock Holmes and Dr Watson Video Series*. London: Longman.

Scarborough D. 1984. *Reasons for Listening*. Oxford: Oxford University Press.

Scott S. and O'Neill R. 1974. *Viewpoints*. London: Longman.

Underwood M. 1971. *Listen to This!*. Oxford: Oxford University Press.

Underwood M. 1976. *What a Story!*. Oxford: Oxford University Press.

Writing

General
Byrne D. 1988. *Teaching Writing Skills.* (New Edition) London: Longman.
Hedge T. 1988. *Resource Books for Teachers: Writing.* Oxford: Oxford University Press.
White R. 1980. *Teaching Written English.* London: Heinemann.

Handwriting
Bright J. and **Piggott B.** 1976. *Handwriting.* Cambridge: Cambridge University Press.
Hartley B. and **Viney P.** 1987. *Learn English Handwriting.* Nashville, TN: Nelson.

Spelling
Burt A. M. 1982. *A Guide to Better Spelling.* Cheltenham: Stanley Thornes & Hulton.
Burton S. H. 1984. *Spelling.* London: Longman.
Evans J. R. 1985. *Spelling Made Easy.* Basingstoke: Macmillan.
Pollock J. 1980. *Signposts to Spelling.* London: Heinemann.

Punctuation
Burt A. M. 1983. *A Guide to Better Punctuation.* Cheltenham: Stanley Thornes & Hulton.
Gordon I. 1983. *Punctuation.* London: Longman.

Speaking – Pronunciation

General
Dickerson W. B. and **Finney R. H.** 'Spelling in TESL: Stress Cues to Vowel Quality', in *TESOL Quarterly*, Vol. 12/2.
Kenworthy J. 1987. *Teaching English Pronunciation.* London: Longman.
Mortimer, C. 1985. *Elements of Pronunciation.* Cambridge: Cambridge University Press.

For contextualized minimal pairs
Baker A. 1981. *Ship or Sheep?.* Cambridge: Cambridge University Press.
Baker A. 1982. *Tree or Three?.* Cambridge: Cambridge University Press.
McLean A. 1981. *Start Listening.* London: Longman.
Trim J. 1975. *English Pronunciation Illustrated.* Cambridge: Cambridge University Press.

Speaking – Communication

General
Kettering J. C. 1975. *Developing Communicative Competence – Interaction Activities in English as a Second Language.* Pittsburgh: Pittsburgh University Press.
Littlewood W. 1981. *Communicative Language Teaching.* Cambridge: Cambridge University Press.

For communicative activities
Hadfield J. 1984. *Harraps Communication Games.* Walton-on-Thames: Nelson.
Hadfield J. 1987. *Advanced Communication Games.* Walton-on-Thames: Nelson.
Klippel F. 1984. *Keep Talking.* Cambridge: Cambridge University Press.
Watcyn-Jones P. 1981. *Pairwork.* Harmondsworth: Penguin.

Games
Astrop J. and **Byrne D.** *Games for Pairwork.* Oxford: Modern English Publications.
Byrne D. 1980. *It's Your Turn – 10 Boardgames.* Oxford: Modern English Publications.
McCallum G. 1980. *101 Word Games.* Oxford: Oxford University Press.
Wakeman A. 1974. *Jabberwocky.* London: Longman.

For problem-solving activities
Maley A. and **Grellet F.** 1981. *Mind Matters.* Cambridge: Cambridge University Press.
Porter Ladousse G. 1983. *Speaking Personally.* Cambridge: Cambridge University Press.

Grammar

Bolton D., **Oscarson M.** and **Peterson L.** 1986. *Basic Working Grammar.* Walton-on-Thames: Nelson.
Eastwood J. and **Mackin R.** 1982. *A Basic English Grammar.* Oxford: Oxford University Press.
Gethin H. 1983. *Grammar in Context.* London: Collins.
Swan M. 1984. *Basic English Usage.* Oxford: Oxford University Press.
Thompson A. J. and **Martinet A. V.** 1986. *A Practical English Grammar.* Oxford: Oxford University Press.
Ur P. *et al.* 1989. *Working with Grammar.* Cambridge: Cambridge University Press.

Vocabulary

Cobb D. 1978. *Puzzles for English Practice – 1, 2 & 3.* London: Longman.
McArthur T. 1972. *Using English Suffixes and Prefixes.* London: Collins.
Seidl J. 1982. *Idioms in Practice.* Oxford: Oxford University Press.
Underhill A. 1980. *Use Your Dictionary.* Oxford: Oxford University Press.
Watcyn-Jones P. 1985. *Test Your Own Vocabulary – Books 1–4.* Harmondsworth: Penguin.

Useful visual material

Bell T. *In Focus – A Visual Resource Book for the EFL Teacher.* Centre for British Teachers Ltd.
Holden S. (ed.) *Materials for Language Teaching – Interaction Packages A & B.* Oxford: Modern English Publications.
Olsen J. W-B. *Look Again Pictures.* Oxford: Modern English Publications.
Wright A. 1984. *1000 Pictures for Language Teachers to Copy.* London: Collins.